CHRIST & QABALAH

OR, THE MIND IN THE HEART

GARETH KNIGHT
※ with ※
ANTHONY DUNCAN

© Gareth Knight & Helga Marshall, 2013

First published in Great Britain in 2013 by Skylight Press,
210 Brooklyn Road, Cheltenham, Glos GL51 8EA

All rights reserved. Except for the quotation of short passages for the purposes of criticism and review, no part of this publication may be reproduced, stored in a retrieval system or transmitted, in any form or by any means, electronic, mechanical, photocopying, recording or otherwise, without the prior consent of the copyright holder and publisher.

Gareth Knight has asserted his right to be identified as the author of this work.

Designed and typeset by Rebsie Fairholm
Publisher: Daniel Staniforth

With very special thanks to Iain Duncan and Helga Marshall for their generous assistance in providing family photographs for this book.

With thanks also to the Rev. Peter Barham for the photographs on p.143 and p.215 (Northern Vicar blog: www.northernvicar.wordpress.com)

Photo on p.86 by M. Blissett
Photo on p.111 by Mick Knapton

www.skylightpress.co.uk

Printed and bound in Great Britain by Lightning Source, Milton Keynes. Typeset in LTC Italian Old Style and Goudy Forum Pro. Poems set in Adobe Caslon Pro.

British Library Cataloguing in Publication Data.
A catalogue record for this book is available from the British Library.

ISBN 978-1-908011-68-8

For Helga
✢

The Reverend Anthony Duncan

Contents

1. Two Brittle Spikes 1930 7
2. Tewkesbury 1964 9
3. Parkend 1965 23
4. Highnam 1969 56
5. Newcastle 1973 85
6. Warkworth 1979 110
7. Whitley Mill 1987 143
8. Corbridge 1995 182
9. Of Toads and Men 2003 214

TWO BRITTLE SPIKES

ME
*Myself (of which I make so great
a fuss) is a mere, brittle spike
of consciousness on the circumference of being;
a tiny terminal of an unplumbed depth.*

*Before I flew, a midnight lark
into the lamplit song, I was a potency;
a tiny "not yet" waiting for the act,
the pre-set accident of chain-reacting love.*

THESE first few lines of a poem by Anthony Duncan sum up the situation in 1930 when I on April 3rd and he on July 28th flew like midnight larks into the lamplit song of life in the world. We had no idea of each other's existence at that time – this was to come thirty-four years later in a narrow window of opportunity when our paths crossed in most unlikely fashion. After which we were seldom out of each other's heads, although never resident in the same part of the country, and living disparate lives.

Prior to that meeting we had followed more or less similar lines. Fairly bright lads who became grammar school boys, if somewhat rebellious and unwilling ones (although with a war on, and many teachers called up, the teaching may not have been the most inspiring). Emerging from school, keen to enter the world of work, but not finding it very fulfilling in a world of post-war austerity when teenagers – in common with television, computers and mobile phones – had not yet been invented, and nearly everything was rationed. So it was not long before he, pushing a pen in an accountant's office, and I, cleaning test tubes in a plastics factory, wondered how to move on, to escape into a wider world.

What better than an equivalent of the traditional ploy of disgruntled youth through the ages, of "running away to sea"? So, despite National Service calling up all eighteen-year-olds, we did not wait for the call to the colours, but blissfully volunteered. He into the army when, after service in Germany and the Far East he wound up as a captain, and I into the air force, when after service in the Middle East I came out as a sergeant.

But during our service a major change came upon each of us, with the force of a revelation. A compelling one at that, yet each of a different type. His, a series of mystical experiences that led him to become a minister in the Church of England. Mine, with almost as great a sense of revelation, coming upon the work of the occultist Dion Fortune and becoming an initiate in the Society of the Inner Light.

By the time we met, he was a newly ordained curate and I was scratching a living in the esoteric world, had written a book on the Qabalah (about to be published), and ran an occult magazine. We were thus inhabitants of two worlds that were never supposed to meet – at least by popular convention – or if they did, to be diametrically opposed to each other.

But, in the words of the poem, being but two brittle spikes of consciousness on the surface of being, of what unplumbed depths were we the terminals? It took the best part of a further forty years to find out. What follows is the story of that encounter.

At an early stage of the game we did wonder whether we should try writing a book together to explain our differences and likenesses but it did not work out that easily. What emerged was a series of books, struck like sparks off each other. And what follows is the closest we have come to joint authorship – but in the end a deep sense of agreement, a channel between two unplumbed depths. The pre-set accident of a chain-reacting love. The sparks between two terminals. The unplumbed depths of Christ and the Qabalah.

Puzzled? So were we when we began. So why not join the dance?

2

TEWKESBURY

My first encounter with the mystical world of Anthony Duncan occurred in the precincts of Tewkesbury Abbey one September day in 1964. It all looked harmless enough – in the form of a little blue poetry book called *Over the Hill* on the abbey bookstall, written by a newly appointed curate.

In my hubris I did not expect to be much impressed by occasional verse of the local clergy, but the first line of one of the poems, *Elmbury Abbey*,[1] caught my eye. "I am fey, so they say…"

Elmbury Abbey

I am fey, so they say;
I have seen the walking dead
Hurry to Mass on a weekday morning.
I have heard the doors go bang
And I have heard their footsteps hurrying.
I have heard the solemn bell's wild clang;
The long, clear call from the tower.

A time and times pass all in one;
The tall stone pillars see, and nod
And see again, and feel a stir
And sense that something must occur
Concerning them, and men, and God.
Signs in the moon and in the sun.

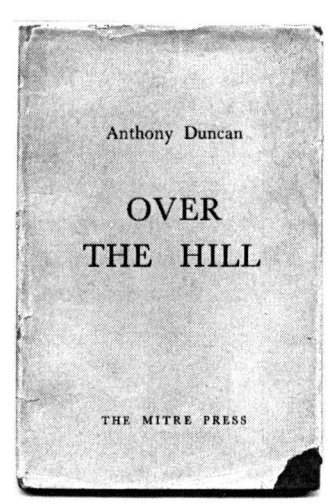

---

[1] Elmbury was another name for Tewkesbury, coined by a popular local author, John Moore, in his evocative *Portrait of Elmbury*. And still to be seen in my day, riding his horse up and down the A38 despite the heavy traffic, and selling his books from door to door when the whim inclined him.

Whoever the writer of this poem was, it seemed that he was unusually psychic, so as the editor of *New Dimensions*, an occult magazine, I felt I would like to be further acquainted, even if he was a local clergyman.

I was not too sure how my own affiliations would go down with a Church of England minister, psychic or not. After all, the magazine I published was pretty forthright in its aims and attitudes and did not seek to hide its light under a bushel. As its first editorial declared:

THE EDITOR THINKS that it is high time that the mystery was taken out of magic, the superstition out of psychism and the pretentiousness out of practical occultism. And this is one thing we hope to do with *New Dimensions*. In these pages we are going to bring occultists, psychics, clairvoyants, palmists, prophets and all the company of esotericism to explain their beliefs and experiences in a sane and rational way to – we hope – a large and sane and rational audience of readers.

Whether such a background and list of intentions would repel rather than attract an abbey curate was very much open to question.

However, I was not averse to making some kind of approach, as before leaving London I had been engaged in a series of talks with the vicar of St. Augustine's, Highgate, with a view to perhaps being confirmed in the Church of England, into which I had been baptised as a child but had had little to do with since. My spiritual affiliations over the past ten years had been somewhat on the other side of the tracks, as a member of a well known occult fraternity, the Society of the Inner Light, which however was by no means anti-Christian.

Since its inception in 1927 by the occultist Dion Fortune, it had pursued a pretty broad-minded way, as a modern equivalent of the ancient Mystery Schools, and for some years before the war had even had a Christian off-shoot open to the public known as The Guild of the Master Jesus. This had fallen by the wayside in the post war period but in 1961 the Society as a whole had taken a sudden shift toward a greater Christian emphasis, encouraged by its Jesuit-educated Warden.

I had not been too enthused by this change, which in the first flush of enthusiasm seemed in danger of changing the role of the Society from Occult School to Religious Sect. But as a member of some eight years standing was content to go along with it in the hope that all would eventually revert closer to the *status quo ante*.

Until to my surprise I received quite a strong personal shove in the Christological direction. Seated in the library one day I was suddenly impressed with the image of Jesus. He seemed to appear and walk a couple of paces toward me and then disappear. It was just a flash of imagination – but so powerful, that to mark the strength of the experience, I got on my motor scooter and went straight out, bought a religious book and recorded the date in the front. The date was 27th September 1961, and the book, selected more or less at random, happened to be *The Imitation of Christ* by Thomas à Kempis.

I cannot say I found its contents by a medieval monk very attractive; it seemed to act more as a talisman than a source of instruction, and in due course I felt prompted to contact the vicar of St. Augustine's, Highgate. It seemed to me it would be no bad thing to go the source of Christian belief and practice to get things straight from the horse's mouth, so to speak.

However, although the high church ambience of St. Augustine's appealed to my esoteric and aesthetic tastes, and the vicar was a sophisticated, intelligent, and charming man of considerable good will, he felt, after some exchange of views, that I was perhaps not quite the type of communicant that the Church of England was looking for. Albeit conceding that I was a most original and fascinating "heresiarch"!

But now, in view of the encouraging sign of picking up the little blue book in Tewkesbury Abbey I felt I might as well try again. And at this point it may be worth recording why I should have happened to be in Tewkesbury Abbey in the first place. For it was the abbey that had originally attracted me to live in Tewkesbury.

Some years before, when doing student vacation work in a local horticultural nursery, I had wandered into Tewkesbury Abbey in the company of my fellow Society of the Inner Light initiate, and later business partner, John Hall. Walking round the abbey as tourists do, John suddenly called to me in some excitement. "Go and sit in there," he said, and pointed to a niche in the west side of the Lady Chapel.

When I did so, I was struck with a most powerful spiritual experience. Nothing visual but an incredibly strong feeling of power and love was focussed there, and seemed unaccountable, except perhaps that the little niche happened to be used as a place for confessions at that time.

Whatever! This caused Tewkesbury Abbey to maintain a magnetic attraction for me – along with a powerful image that kept coming back to me of the abbot at the time of the Wars of the Roses, striding down the aisle to put a stop to Yorkist soldiers slaughtering Lancastrians who had taken shelter there in the aftermath of the Battle of Tewkesbury in 1471. The fields at the back of the abbey are still called the Bloody Meadows.

Another remarkable fact about the abbey is that in 1539 it was saved by the local people from destruction by Henry VIII in his dissolution of the monasteries. Anxious to preserve it as their parish church, they bought it from the king for the then considerable price of £453. There was therefore much love as well as blood associated with the place, and although we may not understand all about the interior dynamics of "place memories", as another poem in the little blue book observed, there was truly a thinness about this place.

Magic

A thin place this,
Where treads my foot more silently;
There is a magic here
Which makes that dark and nail-studded door
That locks dimension from my consciousness
Lean on its bolts in a sudden breeze
And stir my vapid air.

There is a thinness in this place,
Translucent to my senses;
Sensing I know not what
Save that I'm conscious of my hair
And that I breathe, that I can hear
The sound that silence makes
And know a warmth about my face;
And that I walk more slowly home.

At any rate it was this that had caused me, recently, when seeking somewhere to live in Gloucestershire, to light upon Tewkesbury. Happily also finding a congenial 18th century cottage with a walled garden located on the Mythe Tute, a traditional sacred site on the hills immediately north of the town, where my wife Roma and I began to raise a family.

Tewkesbury Abbey

Obviously Anthony Duncan, as author of this kind of stuff, seemed somewhat out of the usual run of Church of England clergy, as indeed it proved from reading the cover of his book.

> The Author of these 24 poems is a priest of the Church of England now serving in the diocese of Gloucester. On leaving grammar school he was articled to a chartered accountant, but disliking office work he left it to join the regular Army, from which, after service in Germany and the Far East, he retired with the rank of captain. Although it was at school that he first commenced to write poetry, he did not commence serious writing until his service in the Far East, where he became deeply influenced by Eastern philosophy and religions; and his poetry is often metaphysical or mystical in character.

So, someone more or less of my own kind, and indeed as it turned out, almost exactly the same age, born within a few weeks of each other in 1930. An ex-grammar school boy, who not taking kindly to the tedium of the world of work, had like me, decamped to join the armed forces – the R.A.F. in my case, although my own service career, being non-commissioned, had been somewhat less elevated in rank, and I retired at the age of 26 as a sergeant rather than a captain.

I thought it best to come clean about the friendly but abortive talks in Highgate when I approached Anthony Duncan in another attempt at dialogue with a minister of religion – and privately to suss out what kind of a man this ex-army clairvoyant might be.

The note I received back seemed quite promising, even flattering, albeit with the veiled hint of an Ace up his sleeve or slid from the bottom of the pack. It all depended on what he meant by "Truth" and "truth".

> From the tone of your letter it seems that perhaps our Lord is drawing you towards the Church which is His "Body", but any confrontation with God is a confrontation with Truth – and we must come to it in truth. There should be plenty to talk about. I look forward to our meeting.

In fact we hit it off pretty well and had plenty to talk about, none of which seemed to throw up any insuperable barrier on either side. Indeed I did begin to wonder at one point whether I was joining not so much the sclerotic institution I assumed the Church of England to be, but rather a congenial construction of Anthony Duncan's own. I should say, though, that he was the most orthodox of clergy. Like C.S.Lewis, whose books of Christian apologetics we both admired, he had a way of putting things across that made them seem both attractive and obvious despite my reservations (and they were many) about the institutional church.

Anyway it came about that after his instruction I was confirmed into the Church of England the following Easter by the Bishop of Gloucester, Basil Guy, to whom I warmed somewhat on hearing his remark that one must expect the Church to be a bit half baked, because it was, after all, run by human beings.

And so for some time things went along quite swimmingly. Although I did find myself appalled after being elected to the Parish Church Council at what I found to be an unholy mixture of ecclesiasticism, incompetence and petty mindedness – which I suppose is what the Bishop of Gloucester must have meant. Still no doubt he and others within the establishment found it possible to live with. No doubt more "christian" than me.

And there was always Tony Duncan to draw some encouragement from. His three kids often provided entertaining diversion in the front pew during church services, no doubt numbed out of their skulls with boredom, with which I felt some sympathy – hymn singing and corporate prayer not being my favourite pastimes. As well as their own couple of boys, he and his wife Helga had adopted a Chinese refugee, a little charmer who went by the name of Fifi – and who was in Roma's class at the local infant school.

They were all attractively a bit off centre. And Helga made no bones about combining her husband's ecclesiastical vocation with being a beauty counsellor or later running a fashion business as a sideline. All in stark contrast with having fled from the Russians in the war. Whilst Tony Duncan's having married a local fräulein while an officer in the British Army of Occupation of the Rhine suggested that he was not afraid to go his own way. Nor was he averse to putting something of his regard for Helga in his little book of poems, which to my mind captured the essence of her.

THE BRUSH

The brush flicks and flashes in the perfumed air,
Blue in the soft lit mirror.
Fussy, fastidious feminine hair,
The exactness of lips,
And the hands, concave like a dancer,
Briefly inspected – then turned and extended;
And I stand there awkward, and dumb for an answer.

Down from the finger nails, perfectly painted,
Down the soft, slender arms, my adoration
Flies and lies snug with the warm little breasts,
Safe and dependent and utterly given;
And my strong arms hold tight
As the little head rests
Childlike and secure in protected protection.

And a later example of light verse exemplified something of the beginnings of that romance:

Yellow Socks

"Some poor bloke's 'ad it Sir! She's knittin' socks!
The little fräulein's 'ard at work in there.
Gor blimey, Sir; you don't 'arf get some shocks!
She's knittin' *yeller* socks to match 'is 'air!"

I laughed politely. We exchanged salutes.
The Sergeant left. I leaned back in my chair
And heard the Army all around; the boots,
The shouts of men, the maleness everywhere.

Incongruous, the thought of knitting pins
And coloured wool within this world of steel.
"Some poor bloke's 'ad it! Sufferin' for 'is sins!"
I smiled, signed Part One Orders; these were *real!*

Were real? The truth transcends this grand design;
Those socks, those golden yellow socks, were mine!

Incidentally, the yellow hair was a figment of the sergeant's imagination. Tony Duncan himself was tall, dark and handsome, and quite imposing in high church cassock or clerical robes, which he used to take great pride in fashioning himself (with or without Helga's help is not recorded) from brightly coloured curtain material. Sometimes the choice of pattern was hardly sacerdotal, as an old lady exclaimed of his cope on one occasion "being all made up of bottles and jugs!"

Another of the poems in his little book interested me not only in the nature of the experience, but what he made of an "absurd confusion of realities".

Ghosts

A cold sweat in the night wind
And a hand of five thumbs fumbling
With a torch button; and a dog cringed
And whimpering.

The man-shape, darker than the night,
Comes weightless over the meadow, cowled
And grave, down to the Abbey
That isn't there.

Candle light in the windows and a
Horse neighing. The guest house stable
Athwart the lamp lit path that isn't there,
Like the dog and the woman.

Clandestine monk who isn't there,
Like the frightened woman and the cringing dog:
Absurd confusion of realities.

And I was also intrigued by what he meant by "over the hill" – the title of one of his poems as well as of the book as a whole.

Over the Hill

I quit the trodden asphalt,
Dusty, bicycled and bare
In the hard midsummer glare.
I quit the lesser Eden,
The council flats and cabbages
And the joyless laughter there,
And I ran away to the deep woods
And the quiet river air.

I found my ease among the trees
That hung the river side;
I listened, still, by the old mill
'Till harness jingled down the breeze,
And then I ran to see them ride
Over the hill, over the hill.

There are two quiet rivers at Tewkesbury, the Avon and the Severn, for they conjoin here. Also an old mill, and quite a famous one too, as, called Abel Fletcher's Mill, it figures largely in the popular 19th century novel *John Halifax, Gentleman* by Mrs. Craik. Whilst the deep woods are also to be found bordering the Severn up on the Mythe hill, the site of my cottage, one of the few places where woad still grows, so beloved by the Celts, back in ancient history.

I wondered if the jingling harness was heard with the physical or the inner ear. Hunts did take place in Gloucestershire but not generally in that location, which is close to the A38 road between Birmingham and Bristol. But I rather thought it might be a level of psychic awareness he was writing about, and not necessarily an historical one, but of the faery folk impinging on the threshold of his consciousness.

The old mill at Tewkesbury

I would have been even more certain about this if I had then had sight of another poem of his that did not appear in the book. A reference to the jungle suggests that this was an earlier experience, when he had been a soldier in the Far East, and at a time when building a little forest shrine might not have seemed so incongruous for a minister of the church.

A Moment Sooner and I Might Have Seen Them...

A moment sooner and I might have seen them
dancing on the mossy floor, or sitting out
under the shade of fungi on tree roots;
but I came crashing through the snapping twigs
and drove them far in sudden fright
through that open door of sunlight
slanting through the dark trunks, deep
in green, mysterious silence.

I have seen
their shadows vanish once before,
under a limestone cliff; leaving
behind a sharp dank incense smell,
brown, green and earthy, as I
crunched heavy on the jungle path.

I will build a little forest shrine;
and they, the squirrel, and the snuffling rat,
and I, shall worship there.

Nonetheless, beneath the urbanity and hail fellow well met exterior of the former army captain was a deeply religious commitment to his priestly duties, as in taking the sacraments through the streets to those unable to attend an abbey service. It was almost possible to envisage himself as one of the ghosts of Tewkesbury, remnants of a bygone age.

Sick Communion

I am a shadow at the edge of dawn;
A silvered shadow, lit by the morning star,
High and alone in the empty sky.
A sky, ragged at the morning's edge,
With day a fitful light
Lifting the foot of its silent curtain;
While heaven stirs
And a cold mist curls on the shadowed earth.

I am a shadow, stirred by the sound
Of an ancient bell. A sound of old
Gold, stroked upon midnight blue.
And I, a Christopher bearing the Christ Child
Under my cloak, go my way
Carrying souls to Bethlehem.

But beyond all this, beyond the psychism, the call of priestly duty, and the observation of his fellow men, was a deep mystical contact of which I, at the time, had little awareness. It was expressed in one of the most deeply personal poems in *Over the Hill* and one which I think few, if any, were likely to comprehend in its significance and mystical reality.

As he later described, the experience came to him when he was in church, an utterly transfiguring experience, when he was caught up high into the air (or so it seemed) and was ravished by Love, and ran from the church in case he should be seen.

My Lover Called Me from the Bed of Dawn

My lover called me from the bed of dawn
And, ankle wet in the heavy grass,
I ran through a curling mist,
Ran to the old stone walls
Of an ancient cell;
And there, in silence heavy with love
As the waking light touched the seraph's wings,
I gave myself to my love.

My love set me down
And was gone on the wings of morning.
I wandered through the early fields
As time returned from a distant tower,
And I looked anew through his dear eyes
And saw his face in every flower.

As he also recorded in a later poem, immediately after such a transcendent experience, his own physical reflection in a mirror shocked him.

Poor Moses

Poor Moses had to veil his face
for he had seen the Lord. Perhaps
he had been seen; a rapture fierce
and all-consuming clawed him up
into a ravishing, his senses burned
like flimsy fuse-wire, lightning-struck.

I know, for I have sudden flared
in rapturous extinction, ultimate embrace;
then tottered back to lodgings, dead.
I have been seen and known, and knew. My face?
I glimpsed it in a mirror – and I fled.

The source of which he revealed as closely as he could in another short poem in his book.

I Am

I am the Dark, the starless void
That claims your closed and searching eyes;
I am the cloud in which you grope
In search of me, in which you rise
Unknowing and in secrecy.

I am the flicker of the lamp.
Now bright, now dark, uncertainly;
I am the blackness of your night
Pierced in a lightning flash of love,
And thus revealed – I am the Light.

However, I did not have the opportunity to get to know Tony Duncan well enough to quiz him much about his psychic or spiritual experiences. If it had been a work of God or of mutual destiny to get us together, it was fashioned in a narrow window of opportunity, for within a few weeks he was appointed Vicar of Parkend, down in the Forest of Dean.

He departed however with a sense of comradeship and fellow service with those who had served the altars here in former times, and perhaps from their place in Paradise may even continue to do so!

Monks of Tewkesbury

And now, my friends in Paradise
(for here is part of Paradise),
as my time comes to go,
a part of me remains with you
to stand on vanished statio
and go, in God, to the Work of God.
Benedicamus Domino.

Comrades in love are you and I;
it shall continue so
until I stand entire at last
who now, on either side of death,
sing the eternal Hours that pass.
There are no more farewells in Christ.
Deo Gratias.

3

PARKEND

Parkend was down in the Forest of Dean, an old town in an ancient forest that lay within a strikingly beautiful stretch of country west of the River Severn and east of the Wye, sufficient to stir both poetic muse and latent nature mysticism in Anthony Duncan. The "thundering bore" in the lines below is a remarkable natural event on the Severn when a concourse of tides in the Bristol Channel causes a tidal wave to roll up as far as Gloucester, and occasionally Tewkesbury and beyond.

West of the Severn

West of the Severn, from Severn to Wye,
A part of me abides.
In from the shore, the thundering bore,
Sandbanks and tricky tides,
From Minsterworth to Huntley, on
Round Longhope, climbing still,
A part of me yet reigns upon
The crowned top of May Hill.

By Yarleton and its old oak
The road winds up and round,
Then climbs a path to mystery,
An earth-ring on the ground.
There sighs the breeze through ancient trees
And young trees planted new.
There, as I please, I take my ease,
My weary heart renew.

West of the Severn, from Severn to Wye,
that part of me will stay
to plead before the Throne of Grace
upon the Judgement Day,
for farming folk and Forest folk
from West of Severn-side;
and they, and I, and ancient oak,
 shall be, and shall abide.

May Hill was a particularly magical place, which he would often visit, not only while at Parkend but at his later incumbency at Highnam, and he returns to it in vision more than once.

May Hill viewed across the River Severn at Framilode

Upon May Hill

Upon May Hill I once would lie.
A hush of trees against the sky,
A silence and a whispering there,
A kinship in the very air.
And I would watch while Severn flowed
Round Arlingham and Framilode,
A shining serpent, silver-spun,
To Bristol and the setting sun,
To Bristol and the setting sun.

Upon May Hill I once would gaze
Far West and North into the haze.
The Sugar-Loaf's arresting stare;
The long, dark line of Marches there;
The Malverns, and the Wrekin's height
At the far limit of my sight.
Then down the Vale of Severn to roam
To Highnam and to thoughts of home,
To Highnam and to thoughts of home.

Upon May Hill I once did dream
And, in a vision, it did seem
An island in a spreading sea.
The Cotswold cliffs they beckoned me,
But far beneath that ocean swell
There muffled rang, as if a knell,
The bells of Gloucester, sounding slow
To wake the world deep-drowned below,
To wake the world deep-drowned below.

And in the last lines of this poem, as in the whole of the one that follows, is a deep level of nature mysticism trying to break through. An innate "elemental faculty" that came naturally to him even in youth and childhood.

May Hill

There is a sacramental something here;
A sighing in the tall trees,
And the grass, alive and whispering;
Speaking to an elemental faculty.

I have known this elemental thing before;
It has caught me helpless, unawares,
Splashing naked in a mountain stream
Or scrambling up through heather on high hills.

It has stunned me with a raging wild desire:
"To be one with this place!
With this hill to be one!"

And left me limp and staring. My sudden spasm
stilled, I've turned and climbed more slowly on.

But here is quietness; the dreadful chasm bridged;
A meeting place, an altar and a fire.

Well, the Forest of Dean, which lies within the country "west of Severn" was certainly a place of deep elemental contacts. A royal hunting forest since the time of the Saxon kings, and source of iron and coal since before the Romans, when the local Dobunni tribe traded iron bars before discovering coinage. Miners from here were used by King Edward I at the siege of Berwick-upon-Tweed in 1296 in his war against the Scots, in recognition of which they were granted free mining rights in the forest, which continue to the present day, along with freedom for any male over the age of 18 to graze sheep within the forest.

Well endowed with oak and beech trees, home to foxgloves and many other wild flowers, plus the presence of boar and deer, the forest is a magical kind of place, as I found very apparent when driving through it after dark, with great ferns overhanging the road. Not a place one would like to break down in, as implied by Tony Duncan when stumbling upon small ancient mine workings – gateways to an underworld as dangerous to fall in psychically as well as physically.

Old Workings

They gape and whisper, beckon from the track,
invoke a trace of terror, lure and fascinate
and suddenly repel. The scratchings and the sombre scars,
the scattered spoil, pockmarks and pits:
faded disfigurements upon a friendly face
wreaked by the venal virus of a ravaged race.

Shades in the shadows rudely beckoned back,
called out of context, in unstable state,
invoked into a borderland that hurts and jars,
seek to identify with a form that fits;
claw blind and clutch – effect the fatal fall
of one to represent the race that caused it all.

INDIGO UNHERALDED

It is a strange, disquieting discovery; almost
embarrassing as if, abroad with hat and coat
and dogs on leash, we stumbled on
the mouth of Hell, mumbled apology
and hurried on. This crater lies
in forest silence, out of business now;
inhabited by ghosts and memories
who, if we're quiet, are not disturbed by us.

The crater curves from crumbling lips
to sudden silence and the night of time.
The stone-lined darkness of an ancient shaft
utters a deep, compelling call;
evokes not past, but present; speaks
of paths to follow, not to fall.

INDUSTRIAL ARCHAEOLOGY

No, not the miseries long past,
The stunted, the exploited lives;
Nor yet the toiling of those hands
That laid the tracks, that dug the deeps.
All these I know. Transmuted now
The ugliness. These things haunt me,
The gentler ghosts: the sleeper stones
Between high, broken, curving banks
Tree-rooted; tumbled walls
And rusted iron, almost gone,
Grassed over and gorse grown;
And long, long silences by ancient shafts
Where mysteries, transcending this poor husk
Of human industry, are almost known,
Half-heard in Earth's own whispering.
These ghosts of daylight are my friends;
I do not linger after dusk.

Apart from any elemental powers, the forest had its lawless side in the human realm, when from medieval to early modern times ragged wretches eked out a living in poor housing, without sanitation, overlord or Poor Law relief. Living in a royal hunting forest was not allowed, but the presence of iron ore, stone and timber made it a tempting target for those struggling to exist on its boundaries, squatting in hastily constructed shacks and then moving on. The occultist William Gray had a theory that local faery lore had its origin in the small dark aboriginal forest dwellers who dwelt here, quite capable of robbing, killing or carrying off to their dark pits any hated official or wandering stranger.

But in the early 19th century Parkend became an important industrial village, with coal mines, iron works, stone works, tinplate works, timber yard and even a stretch of railway line. Then in the early 20th century decline set in, leaving it now to scratch a living from the tourist trade.

St Paul's church, where Tony Duncan was now vicar, had been built in 1822 at the beginning of this era of prosperity, under the aegis of a local worthy, the Reverend Henry Pool, who having had some previous experience in an architect's office, produced a church on an unusual octagonal plan. He may have got his ideas from late 18th century Methodist churches, although I thought it quite a magical layout myself.

Interior of St Paul's church, Parkend, with its unusual octagonal layout

Tony Duncan, in recognition of its Welsh connections (after the Romans left, the land west of Severn may have been part of the Welsh kingdoms of Gwent and Ergyng) chose to call his new church Llanfihangel – place of the angel – in a poem which contains in its final lines a hint of his ministry of exorcism, of which more later.

LLANFIHANGEL
[St Paul's Church, Parkend]

It was the place of angels glimpsed, half-seen,
Half-fleeting in the corners of unheeding eyes;
A stillness all around, a spiralling in Light,
Transcending roofs and grey stone walls,
Invoking love, by Love Himself invoked
In setting forth the Victory. To know,
To see, to understand in part
Wounds both the feet and hands, and breaks the heart.

And he found a quiet place for meditation in a far corner of the vicarage garden. As he later recorded: "The forest was on two sides; it was like a frontier post. I wanted to build a little hut for meditation and silence, and 'being myself' in. It seemed to be a kind of threshold to another world."

THE OLD ORCHARD

Here is my quiet corner, one might call it a glade,
tree and moss and wild-flower filled; here I
shall build my castle, there the stones shall be laid.
So shall I raise it up to the leafy sky
and reign there silent, sorrowful and sage,
while mysteries are opened, magic made;
while barren fruit-trees of advancing age
extend their frail embarrassment, and shade.

Here, with a royal joy and an infinity of sorrow,
these eyes will seek to blaze through stick and stone
and, with the seer, see and see and know –
and find that long-suspected thing was ever so.
Here is my quiet corner, one might call it a throne,
and here I reign today, and there tomorrow.

Meanwhile the Duncan family were cheerfully down to earth, culling the blackberry bushes rampant in the old churchyard, for Helga to make into Bramble Jelly, that the children merrily called "Resurrection Jam". And delicious it was too, spread on Helga's home made bread!

It was here in Parkend that over the next four years Tony Duncan began a serious study of the Qabalah, on the strength of a book I sent him – my long awaited and newly published two volume work *A Practical Guide to Qabalistic Symbolism*. I sent it rather speculatively as a follow up to explain some of the esoteric references I had made in our earlier discussions at Tewkesbury.

To my surprise he wrote back almost immediately to say how much he had enjoyed reading it, and that at least I had rescued the subject from sensational occult novels, like those of the immensely popular Dennis Wheatley.

A few weeks later he wrote to say that he had read it all through again and was becoming quite enthusiastic. It seemed to him that the Qabalah was a remarkably profound thing and most profitable field of study – particularly for him. He thought it a great pity that it was virtually unknown, largely because of its own esoteric pretensions; or where it was known, hugely misunderstood as something weird and macabre.

He did have some reservations though, particularly with Volume II, which rather heavily featured Tarot card symbolism.

> I am picking my way through Vol II rather as one does through gorse! I never had a head for cards, and the Tarot, although fascinating and probably worth a long look one day, seems almost as bewildering and shark infested an occupation as playing Rummy with Great-aunt Nelly and Great-aunt Jean!

He did, however, in later years, change his assessment of the Tarot, and came to recognise it as a remarkable set of archetypal principles.

I could not at this stage quite fathom what his reservations about the Qabalah were – which he described in these terms:

> The thing is, of course, to put it in its right place... The Light of Christ is hidden under a Qabalistic bushel, and man is imprisoned within his philosophy. But put the Qabalah under the light of Christ and, my word, it is a damn fine bushel!

Anyhow, at my suggestion, he bought a copy of *Psychosynthesis* by Roberto Assegioli, a psychologist who, rather like C.G.Jung but even more so, had gone to esoteric sources to formulate a system of psychotherapy.

On the other hand he had to spend some time batting off criticisms by me of the established Church, now with experience of the inside as well as the outside, and some blistering disillusionment at what I found to be an ill-chaired, rambling, reactionary, petty minded meeting of the Parish Church Council. On a broader front this was a period of considerable turmoil, as the Church tried to redefine itself in the cultural revolution of the 1960s. "No small change" was the title of a kind of internal missionary effort to encourage serious "stewardship" of church members by contributing more systematically to its dwindling coffers than dropping their small change into the collection plate. At the same time there was much stir about ecumenism, with much agonising over the validity of holy orders from one denomination to another – Anglican, Methodist, Baptist let alone Roman Catholic – which to my mind seemed much like the politicking between rival bureaucracies at the prospect of a business merger, larded with a layer of "holier than thou" one-upmanship. Added to which was a fit of "the liturgical fidgets" introducing one form of service after another in an attempt at "relevance" for modern man – who did not seem to care all that much anyway – at risk of upsetting the traditional faithful deprived of their familiar prayer books.

Tony Duncan was quite sympathetic to my disillusionment (and used to refer to reading the *Church Times* as his weekly penance).

> Talking of babies and bathwater – I rate "churchianity" as rancid bathwater... One of the horrid things about what the masters call the Purgative Way is the crashing boredom of "religion", the manifest dotage of ecclesiastics, and the interminable gloom of "services"; all the kicks have vanished into the night. And if I may say so, Oh!, how I suffered in just that period! But it is a clearly marked path on the spiritual map (visible to others rather than oneself of course) and if steadfastly trod, it issues in the end in the beginnings of spiritual maturity and real humility. (Oh! What a nasty dig – but I am quoting from the book – and have suffered.) Babies and bathwater; remember who the baby is.

No doubt he had in mind early experiences of his own on the well trodden path of the mystic.

Aches and Pains

I ache for God; a dry, a hollow pain
Which runs along beneath my every day,
Cries for relief, seeks fretfully a way
To be articulate, but seeks in vain.
I ache. My fretfulness is but a drain
Which drains me dry. I grope for words to say
But am struck dumb, my wits fled far away.
So I abide – and ache, and ache again.

I ache for God. I recognize my case
As hopeless for the Hope in which I stand.
I ache, and ache the more for words to bring.
One Word alone abides. No time, no space.
The ink runs dry, the pen breaks in my hand.
For of the Imageless can no man sing.

CONTEMPLATION

Come dark, come daylight; and the longest hour
From Mattins bell which signalled my resolve
Until the tower clock should signal my release
Ate rust and iron into my very soul.

My feet were fastened in the stocks of prayer;
An hour-long thrash for shreds of recollection,
Year-in, year out. The memory of it mocked
My scrambled silences, invited to despair.

So time passed into timelessness, how many years?
From Mattins 'til the clock struck off my chains
A trackless desert, dry, too parched for tears,

'Til I acclimatised to that accursed land
And met my Lord there. Meeting quite absurd;
We nodded, smiled, and passed without a word!

But as for the church as a whole he remained blithely optimistic.

> As a matter of fact, one of the quite wildly exciting things about living now is the steady rediscovery of the true nature of the Church. That is the "ground swell" that is producing all this tedious froth on the surface. The Church is not and never was "the nation at prayer" – not even in the Old Testament… Roman Legalism is the trouble (by Roman I don't simply mean "Roman Catholic" – although they have it even worse then we have). It is a Western European attitude of mind which would tidily devise a nice set of rules applicable to all persons at all times. Total conformity. It is a thousand miles from the mind of Christ who is far too big for that kind of nonsense. It leads, if unchecked, to a "professionalism" which equates the Church with her clergy…
>
> But the Holy Spirit has us by the scruff of the neck and incredible things are happening. The dry as dust quibble over Orders that gives more people than you the creeps will fade away, as it were. The truth of the quibble will "out" as truth always does. The Holy Spirit is better at "outing" it than we are. There is an infinity of space in Christ for lone and specialised paths – and all the more so in the West. I wouldn't live in any other age for all the "teh" in China. (sorry!)

He took issue with some of the "tedious froth" in a paperback book of his that shortly appeared. I found the title – *Pray and Live* – not exactly enticing but it was apparently wished upon him by the publishers, the Society for the Propagation of Christian Knowledge (SPCK). The book was Tony Duncan's reaction to an immensely popular book of three years before, *Honest to God*, by John Robinson, Bishop of Woolwich. This had caused great controversy by saying that God could no longer be imagined as a grandfatherly figure "up there in the sky" or "out there somewhere" but ought rather to be regarded as "the ground of our being." Which was all a bit too abstract and trendy for many of the faithful.

Tony Duncan rose to the challenge not by setting out a "new" approach to God but by reverting to an old one. Based upon a 14th century spiritual guide, *The Cloud of Unknowing*, he evoked the so called "negative way" of affective and contemplative prayer. That is to say, seeking a personal relationship with God as a pure Being beyond any image or form. Not that this, despite its merits, I thought likely to cut much ice with the average churchgoer.

But with its roots in Neoplatonism, it was a tradition that had inspired generations of Christian mystics, including the Jesuit priest and scientist Pierre Teilhard de Chardin, whose sweeping account of the unfolding of the cosmos, *The Phenomenon of Man*, caused something of a sensation when it appeared in 1959. I recall it being enthusiastically received by the Warden of the Society of the Inner Light, and it had obviously also made quite an impression upon Anthony Duncan, as shown in his next book, published in 1968, entitled *The Whole Christ*.

The underlying theme of this book was to see humanity as "the spearhead of the cosmos", the final fruit of the first stage of the evolution of consciousness, that had started with the formation of hydrogen atoms in space, and continued through the whole of evolutionary development of organic and human life until destined to be brought to perfection and summed up "in Christ". A process from "alpha" to "omega". Within the background of this vast cosmic setting, Tony Duncan asked us to look at the nature and purpose of the Church as "the body of Christ", in a process of becoming the "whole Christ".

He had indeed summed up much of this in one of the poems that appeared in *Over the Hill*.

NIRVANA POINT
"The ceasing of becoming is Nirvana." Buddha S.N.ii.68

Becoming is falling;
A falling out of knowledge into darkness.
Darkness is not the negation of light
But a condition of it. As darkness grows
So grows the knowing which is love;
The true knowing, growing as the being shrinks
And journeys to Nirvana Point;
The end of all becoming.

Our being falls towards this point
Where all the lines converge
And funnels terminate.
Nirvana Point, shaped like a cross;
The spinning coin whose heads is light
And tails darkness. The lens and shutter
Of the cosmic camera, whose fitful click
Flashes an image on the soul's pin-point
As it hurtles down in its light tight box.

Alpha and Omega. We fall from one
Towards the other, our antipodes.
Pilgrims, we pass the iron gates
Of our Nirvana, where becoming
Is fulfilled; where falling turns
To soaring, in the one straight line –
Alpha to Omega; and both are one.

However, whatever the merits of *The Whole Christ* as a fascinating edifice of cosmic speculation, the practicalities of *Pray and Live* did not have a great impact upon me. Having followed a discipline of occult meditation for a good many years I did not feel that I needed any instruction in this kind of thing. But Tony Duncan and I still had a lot to teach each other that neither of us quite realised as yet.

He was currently busy coming to terms with the contents of my book, and tended at first to approach the Qabalah on a psychological basis, reporting that "after floundering about" in Assigioli and others he could see that the Qabalah was a jolly good chart of the human personality, and deserved to be more widely known. And to this end he intended to write a book about it.

In response to this I was happy to supply him with esoteric reading material from the stock of Helios Book Service. This ranged from Olive Pixley's *The Armour of Light* (which he found "somewhat odd") to Aleister Crowley's *Magick in Theory in Practice* ("remarkable but unutterably *sad*"), but in addition to my own book he found best instruction from Dion Fortune's *Mystical Qabalah* and the first 22 lessons of the *Helios Course on the Practical Qabalah* that I had commissioned, and which was currently being written by the occultist and Liberal Catholic priest, W.E.Butler.

Not that Tony Duncan confined his studies to modern Qabalists; he also turned to *Major Trends in Jewish Mysticism* by Professor Gerhart Scholem ("who is slightly shirty about Gentile Qabalists!").

And within six months he had written three preliminary essays, one on *Gnosis and Gnosticism*, one on *The Qabalah in Jewish Mysticism*, and one *Concerning Magic* which made a vital distinction between Magic and Mysticism – a point by no means always realised, and at first by neither of us. He added:

> I am pretty clear about what my position is about the whole business of the Qabalah. It will take a book to explain it, but while I have become conscious of the big snags – and there are a few, and some pretty fundamental – I am quite convinced that there is a great mine of useful, indeed very valuable stuff here, well mixed about with much that is less valuable – or in some cases, value nil. I think I can be both objective and fair about this and I am quite sure that the job is very well worth doing.

He called the book *The Christ, Psychotherapy & Magic* the manuscript of which eventually turned up on my desk after being rejected by a bemused SPCK on the grounds that they could not think of any reviewer qualified to pass an opinion on it!

However, during its gestation, a number of points of difference arose between us, bringing various misconceptions, misunderstandings, and obscured issues into stark relief. Much of this came about by my sending him the draft of a couple of little monographs I had written, one called *Occult Exercises and Practices* and the other *The Practice of Ritual Magic*. Rather to my surprise it was the first of these, rather than the second, that brought a startled and negative reaction from him.

Occult Exercises and Practices had been inspired by a classic title of the 1920s, *Your Psychic Powers and How to Develop Them*, a comprehensive 380-page volume by the distinguished psychical researcher Dr Hereward Carrington. Virtually unobtainable at the time (although frequently reissued since) I would have published it myself if I had had the money, but compromised by bringing out a little 68-page monograph of my own. It aimed to be a complete beginner's guide to practical occultism, describing exercises in the development of clairvoyance, clairaudience, relaxation, meditation, magical visualisation, with the addition of a couple of chapters on spiritual exercises and prayer.

Much of this Tony Duncan reckoned to be badly off course – and said that parts made his hair stand on end!

> Have just read through *Occult Exercises and Practices*. Rather a lot of comment on the first few pages! There are some major misunderstandings, an "oo-er" or two and a few "gor-blimeys", and I think some of these really ought to be put straight.

But aiming to be constructive he asked what was the end in view? The key question being, what is the intention of the performer? Why is he trying this? For kicks, for power, out of curiosity? The dangers of delusion and morbid auto-suggestion were considerable in some of them. Others – such as influencing people – seemed quite illicit, whilst trying to recall past incarnations might be good clean fun – if you were a Hindu and believed in that kind of thing! (He plainly did not at this time, although he later revised his views.)

Whilst I recognised the validity of some of what he said I went ahead with publication anyway. All my own acquaintance with the subjects under review had been ethically practised and I saw no point in concealing what were facts of nature. Most things are open to abuse but ignoring or concealing them seemed no good way to deal with them.

However, he had been working hard at evaluating the various expressions and assumptions of the esoteric student, some of which he rendered into verse, and many years later collected into a little photocopied booklet called *The Great Work*. One or two were directly related to Qabalistic meditation on aspects of the Tree of Life:

KABBALAH

I have touched the fringes of *Kether*
in rising, raptured, on the inner planes;
I have centred me on *Tifareth*
in knowledge of the guardian there;
I have ransacked the Tree of Life
in search of its forbidden fruit.

My Quest for Meaning and for Truth
brought me full-circle to *Malkhuth*
where I received in bread and cup
the first-fruits of the Kingdom

PATH-WORKING

To walk the paths upon the Tree of Life
Is to explore a hidden, inner realm
Of archetypes and old, uncertain gods.
Tread warily and with respect. And why
And with what motive is this journey made?

With map and guide-book in his eager hand
The rambler may roam, amused, detached,
The natives, it is hoped, are friendly here
And local guides are sometimes to be found.

The Inner Plane Entrepreneur, alert,
Acquisitive, finds much that opportunes.
Prime, plump young powers for the picking here!

The tourist, fascinated, comes again, again;
They both pollute the outer and the inner plane.

To an Urgently Aspiring Mystic

Cross-legged you sit, with spine erect, and head
As hollow as a bell. Who rings within?
What Kabbalistic pathways do you tread,
What images or archetypes to bring?

Or have you overpassed the great Abyss
And, crowned and Macrocosmic now, bide still;
Embodied but transcendent? And what bliss
Of introspection with no Time to kill!

No, fellow-traveller, I do not mock!
Beware the mystic spiral lest it turn
Upon itself. For I have passed this way
And taken many turnings, known much shock:
Humiliation as the Ego burns
When Grace alone redeems the errant Stray.

Two Dimensions

In two dimensions was my understanding bound;
I pigeon-holed my knowledge on the Tree of Life
And ironed my perceptions flat, ring-fenced
My possibilities and took the road-map for the real.

A long time since. The Tree is now set free
From fuss and fret-work. Knowledge is gone away
Fulfilled, released, and happy in redundancy.

And a need to burst out from this kind of confinement to direct mystical experience.

THE GNOSTIC

I seek for knowledge? No. I seek the Lord,
And all the rest is added unto me
To be grown out of lest it fascinate;
Lest lost in nuts and bolts I lose my Way.

Knowledge shall fade away in Understanding;
Give place at last to Holy Wisdom
Which is all Compassion. This is the state
Of one who would be called along Christ's Way.

THE SEEKER

All this my seeking, mind in heart;
To know, to comprehend. A curiosity of Love.
My *gnosis* is my Love, my Living Lord;
I climb the esoteric Tree of Life

Within the context of His Sacred Heart
And rise by Grace upon the planes of prayer,
Heart-broken daily, having died and died
To all but the Compassion of the Crucified.

To reach beyond all knowing and to understand,
And then in Silence in the Holy Wisdom fall:
The consummation of an Everlasting Love;

The Quest of Man in whom, for whom, I strive,
Stirring the Vortex, turning inside-out
Until all's passed away and gone – and all's alive!

And in this next one, rather like St Paul before him, presenting in the third person an experience that happened to himself.

I Know a Man...

I know a man caught up, caught up,
I know not where, what Heaven's height;
All out of Time, and given sight.

And there were given him forbidden things;
The love of living flames, bronze, burning bright,
And holier men than he shall be, all wondrous white.

He lingered there full twice ten thousand years
Until released, intoxicate with Light,
To kneel upon his knees again in Earth's own night.

And here he gives an indication of an idea he was to develop later, of a difference between "inner space" and "inner planes" – the first referring to a direct mystical approach to God, the latter to the investigation of the inner side, or "nuts and bolts", of the Creation.

Understanding

The Inner Planes are part of Inner Space,
Contained, as is this outer Earth, to line
Earth's each dimension and at their every point.

The Inner Space transcends, contains
The Outer; is dimensionless and "other" and beyond;
And is the proper ambience of Contemplation.

The Inner Planes of outer Earth
Are bounded by its aura. Here the mind
Can reach, and this the realm of Meditation.

Yet Inner Space transcends it all, directionless.
The heart is Man's own lodestone, and who yearns
Beyond imagining shall touch God's own Imagination.

Meaning

I am blinded by the nuts and bolts of things;
bewildered by immensity. Imagination, blasted,
lies in ruins at unending strings of numbered noughts,
this way and that, to make all meaning meaningless.

Yet, god-like though created, I transcend all that;
the mathematics in my mind, I over-reach the stars
and know about them, and begin to understand
the shape of my dominion in a wider land.

All this *without*, as seen by mortal eyes
upon one plane of being, one face of things.
What lies *within?* The love of persons is the key

to every lock, the handle of each heavy door,
of every place and plane the plan; eternally the Way
through never-ending weary worlds to what bright skies?

We were beginning, in fact, to realise the difference between the occultist and the mystic, a point that he was to bring out in *The Christ, Psychotherapy and Magic*. And the fact that I was one and he was the other effected a great mind clearing, in our view of where each other stood. Both were quite valid pursuits of rather different aims.

But in the meantime our differences came to something of a crisis after a conversation which mentioned in passing the ministry of exorcism in which, with the Anglican Benedictine monk, Dom Robert Petitpierre, he was occasionally engaged.

It triggered a very vivid dream for me immediately afterwards. In the dream it seemed that a church needed to be exorcised, and I was asked to help and went along with him. He was dressed in his vestments as for the mass, and I came in my magical robes. When we arrived, the Bishop of Gloucester was already in the place carrying out an exorcism – with all hell let loose inside! There were also, it seemed, one or two other Christian priests and a number of laity about the place.

We both stood outside the door, about to go in, but discussing whether it was advisable for me to wear my magical robes in case others present might not understand, and be alarmed by them. I remembered feeling a little exasperated at this because magical robes would be by far the most effective and appropriate for me to wear. However I just recall agreeing to go in wearing a black cassock only (a kind of disguise as a deacon I suppose!) and then all faded from consciousness.

In writing about this to Tony Duncan I wondered if it might perhaps have been recall of an actual astral experience.

He wrote back to say he thought the dream highly significant, and that it said something rather clearly. My magical robes had to be discarded in order for the dress of a servant to be put on ("deacon" means "servant"). Immediate texts about "putting off the old Adam" etc., came to mind, but the main point was that one had to discard the role of being a manipulator (for want of a better term). One has to cease being one who "does things" and become instead one through whom things may be done by Christ *if He so chooses*.

It was ever a contention of Tony's, I think somewhat ambivalent about his own psychic sensitivity, that one should never *seek* to use these powers, but wait to see if one was *called* to use them by higher authority. Although I have to say that this had always been the crux of my own magical activities, taken for granted as a result of my rigorously ethical esoteric training

He suggested that there might come a time when I realised that some of my activities were no longer compatible with a Christian profession. He was sure I must know this, just as I must know that the devil works by compromise and subtlety.

This was a bit too much for me to swallow! I wrote back to say I was somewhat surprised and disappointed to find him indulging in a bit of amateur psychoanalysis on my behalf, and it seemed to me that more light was being thrown on the neurosis of the analyst than that of the analysed. The thing that particularly bothered me was his preoccupation with insinuations of the devil, which seemed at times to verge on "old maid's insanity". I got the impression – I hoped wrongly – that I stood a good chance of being cast in the role of the serpent offering the poisoned, or forbidden fruit. And if this was the case then it would seem to put paid to any hope of fruitful communication between us.

He wrote back immediately asking me not to be too upset by his "psychoanalysis". Perhaps it was an impertinence, but he felt the principles were right – although he was ready to concede that the sanctions he mentioned were not applicable in my case – and that I felt a distinct vocation to the occult as a Christian. It was this mutual acceptance on both our parts that had been so productive and mind clearing so far and likely to continue to be so. Was it not the vocation of both of us to bring this whole business into the light of day? So far as it lay in us to do so, to see it for what it was – with God glorified in it, and a whole very profound area of life fulfilled and redeemed. We each had a "frontier" to guard along with a clear sense of vocation.

As for the devil! His main delight was subtly preventing people from being themselves, from following their vocations, and from being what the adult Christian *must* be – fully free and responsible in Christ. He had at times insinuated himself into the "institutional church" and one of the things he promoted was Ecclesiasticism and another was Churchianity. Both were abominations, and in both he sometimes deceived the very elect. What is more, a crisis at present to be found in the enclosed religious orders was caused by the tension between growth into full responsibility and the idea (appropriate to a former age, but not this one) of unquestioning obedience.

Anyway, I should not be too worried by his preoccupations with the devil! I should be assured that I did not look a bit like him! That thought at least had made him laugh out loud. However, it might just be (please allow the possibility – at least in principle) that he had insights and objective experience which – dare he say it – I had not! In aspects of the priesthood which he was not at liberty to discuss (and for which he could find no words if he could) he was left in no doubt whatever of the reality of certain dangers. Perhaps he had been projecting onto me his own tensions and it was *his* integrity he had to watch. This was *his* battle, *his* tension, and he had to resolve it in order to fulfil a vocation which was as clear to him as mine was to me, to subject occultism to the light of Christ.

This tension was caused by his occasional calling to a ministry of exorcism (of which he could only speak in the most superficial way) and there was a connection, sometimes at any rate, between the "troubles" dealt with therein and occult practices. And it was a very clear part of his vocation – albeit a branch line of it – to become clear about the nature of this connection.

Although this line of vocation was not one that he cared to talk about, he did, over the years, reveal some aspects of it in his poetry.

An Exorcism

"I hope you won't be shocked," she said,
with honest eyes, twisting her gloves
between unconscious, nervous hands.
There is no shocking any more;

all pain is gathered up, all borne
in one eternal painfulness;
the universe a running sore
made whole, the iron bands

that bound it, broke; all loves
made one in Love; all dead
alive. The good and evil twist
and turn within the exorcist

'til with Christ's love his heart runs red.
"I hope you won't be shocked," she said.

This poem was referred to, in passing, in a later work of his, in the views of an angelic figure.

> "That girl had dignity and your compassion was aroused by it. She did not conceal the shame she felt. She was utterly honest and you, a priest, loved her for it. So does God love man. So he changed his Mind, just as you changed your mind. He responded, just as you responded. God is not a machine, and neither are you."

Another poem described the following incident.

Joy in Heaven

They were angry when we walked across their grave
and followed us. They led us to their room
and took their places, set each on a chair
where they had sat, four hundred bitter years,
and filled both house and garden with despair.

And so the four of us held parliament,
and street lights cast long shadows on the floor,
'til love broke through four centuries of pride
and brought them down to lay their secrets bare;
to tell his murder, tell her suicide.

Melchizedek, he brought forth bread and wine
for priest he was, and pleading as he did,
the host of heaven rode in upon the rite,
set flame about that still, that silent pair,
and bore them homeward on a blaze of light.

What was the moment of truth for those two ghosts to whom he ministered, he later pondered, and reflected:

> I think there were two moments of truth in each case. In the case of the murderer, it was first the moment of consent to the temptation to commit the grave sin – a sin against his own integrity as well as against the victim. Second, the moment of truth – the real one – was the solemn facing of that fact in penitence after four hundred years. For the suicide it was much the same. Earthly death had not radically altered their situation.

Another poetically recorded incident seemed one of ancient magical practice, of binding souls for personal use, even in the precincts of a church. And which has an intriguing final stanza, that raises more questions than it answers.

THE CHARMED RING

Two worlds in time, but separate in time,
And one half-timeless yet and unresolved;
A circle bound the three of them. Within,
Long buried, three young victims lie.

Half-bound and half-awake they lay. To die
Reluctant messengers, to be manipulate
As tools of power for a fell, dark mind
Long dead and decomposed, their lot.
To leave for other men to find
This place a hallowed but unquiet spot.

Three victims in an everlasting youth
Are dancing. And a fourth, in time,
Sits reading in a stall. The ring is broke,
The circle vanished in the Uncreated Light.

I was that reader. With God's gift of Sight
I saw the fire of love within her eyes
Who danced between two partners; the surprise
And joy upon her face, her flaxen hair.
And in my heart I danced into the Light,
For I would know her, and shall know her, everywhere.

There are other events that speak of more conventional hauntings, oftentimes discernible only to the more psychically sensitive, but at other times breaking through into the realm of normal consciousness.

Personally I was quite content to leave this kind of thing to him and to those appropriately qualified; I had never felt ghost-busting to be part of my vocation. Although I have had my occasional brushes with psychic unpleasantness, as on an occasion when some occultists who should have known better took exception to my work with Anthony Duncan. He referred to it soon after, choosing fairly light hearted terms.

> I am not surprised at the repercussions of the weekend. I had expected more and worse. Nevertheless on the night 30th April, we were all wakened up by mocking voices, to discover "watchers" all over the place and a lot of very dark darkness about. It was not too bad, having discovered it, as the angels, once invoked, swept it all up nicely. But forewarned is forearmed and the next night we said our prayers in advance and I was woken up almost as if to hear some very neat angelic stroke play, as a very fierce assault indeed was played smartly to the boundary. One could almost HEAR it bouncing off! After that, all has been sweetness and light, but I wonder if anyone had bad twinges the next day!

It seems that the occasion, or some later consequences of it, called for some comment in verse, in somewhat more sombre terms.

THE CURSE

Ill-wishes working weird within,
by you unknown, unnoticed; nor
the perpetrators and their sin
suspected. What had gone before
forgotten, unremembered quite.
But others bitterly resent
the very things you represent
and stabbed in horrid, hidden spite.

I took the blow, such was my place,
and silent bled the live-long day,
unknowing, 'til at last, by Grace
I understood, half ebbed away.
With all made plain and all revealed,
the curse was lifted. My own part:
to hold you deep within my heart
for Love's sake, that we both be healed.

As mentioned before, somewhat to my surprise he found no difficulty with my other little book *The Practice of Ritual Magic*, which was a short manual based on the work of the occultist W.G.Gray whose introduction to the Qabalah, *The Ladder of Lights*, and major work *Magical Ritual Methods*, I had published. I had sent both along to Tony Duncan to add to his reading list and he said he had found much "very head-clearing stuff" in them.

Indeed, after I had introduced him to the little temple, based on W.G.Gray's methods, that I had built at the bottom of my garden, he responded in very positive terms.

> As a matter of fact, the most convincing argument you ever employed in defence of your vocation was that implied in your showing me the shed in your garden! I felt quite at home. I find it hard to conceive anything in the truest sense "unlawful" having gone on in there.
>
> Yes, your oratory is a religious place – I prefer the expression, a holy place – because it is devoted to the devotional practice of magic IN CHRIST. IN CHRIST, the symbolism was meaningful; truths were expressed therein within the context of him who IS Truth. It is plain to me that our Lord has not been leading you to himself through magic

either for fun or for your own private benefit. I think a realisation of his most all-embracing remark "I came not to destroy, but to fulfil" is involved here. It is a pity that almost no clergy either know a thing about this, or else they have encountered a perversion of it, and have had to clean up the resulting mess. There is no doubt in my mind, and this is amply supported by my own experience and that of others, that objective evil can "ride in" upon the practices of occultism – but the INTENTION of the operator is all-important, as is made clear in most of the books I have consulted. I am sure that it is our Lord's will that this whole field should be redeemed and made whole and subjected to his Light. I am equally sure that the time was not ripe until about now... Alas! The only other clerics known to be interested are known nut-cases and cranks! (Perhaps I am! But no, there is a vocation here, I am sure of it.)

I cannot find any reason to doubt your own sense of vocation in this. It seems to me that this must be done IN CHRIST which is what is happening. There is more to the life of Holy Church, and more flowing out from her altars, than parochial ecclesiasticism dreams of! (But even that has its place – the high-road within the Body of Christ.)

Anyhow, a clear and considered statement of where he stood as a result of our conversations, correspondence and the books I had lent him arrived on my desk early in 1969 in the form of a book length manuscript, *The Christ, Psychotherapy & Magic*. And I was quite touched to read in the Author's Preface:

> This book is, in part at least, a small act of reparation for a lost pastoral opportunity. A soul for whom Christ died did not receive the help and guidance appropriate to his condition because the writer was in total ignorance of the subject-matter of this book. This ignorance is shared, it may be confidently asserted, with fully nine-tenths of the writer's clerical brethren.

Anyway he made up for it later! We continued to strike sparks off each other and to discover greater depths in each other's position than we ever suspected at first.

A great deal of the book was quite familiar to me, as the central part consisted largely of quotations from Dion Fortune's *The Mystical Qabalah* and my own *A Practical Guide to Qabalistic Symbolism*. This was in line with the book's subtitle and general intention as *A Christian Appreciation of Occultism*.

His own views and conclusions were contained in the final third of the book under the heading *The Search for Self-Realization*. What had caused him most difficulty was getting to grips with a "theology" of the occult, for as he came to realise, it was not so much a religion, but rather a huge range of teaching and practice containing all kinds of religious speculation, some of it quite contradictory.

And no doubt oriental influence had been very extensive, largely through the Theosophical Society in the late 19th and early 20th centuries.

He found it most easily approached in terms of Jungian psychology or the *Psychosynthesis* of Roberto Assegioli, in which the Qabalistic Tree of Life could be of considerable value as a framework of symbolism or pattern of archetypes. A coherent and generally credible guide to what he felt must surely be the structure of the Collective Unconscious.

I have to say that I had my doubts about interpreting esoteric experience in terms of psychology. Certainly in the early 1930s Jung caused quite a stir in esoteric circles by beginning to take "forbidden" subjects like alchemy seriously, and many occultists, including Dion Fortune and Israel Regardie, welcomed this initiative as seeming to give some scientific respectability to occultism. However, over the years this optimistic assessment began to cool off. As far as I was concerned, a great deal of what we called "the inner planes" could not be confined within the human psyche, individually or collectively; there were objective realms hidden (or "occulted") behind physical appearances, and just as "real" and extensive as the material universe.

However, to his credit, Tony Duncan was not seeing it in quite such reductionist terms, for he saw it as a link to his own theological position, aided and abetted with insights from Teilhard de Chardin's *The Phenomenon of Man*. Thus the term "collective unconscious" was capable of much wider application. It embraced a whole process of evolution of consciousness from the hydrogen atom in inter-galactic space to the phenomenon of man. On these terms the "collective unconscious" could be regarded as the *within* of the created order, or what Tony Duncan liked to call "the psychic nuts and bolts" of the inside of Creation.

Thus he felt that the occult could, like science, have a valid and important place – not as an alternative religion, but as an empirical investigation of the created order. This was not to devalue occultism, but simply to see it in its proper place, in which the Tree of Life of the Qabalah was a useful pragmatic device, a kind of map or flow chart to serve as a reasonable exploratory guide. Occultists such as Dion Fortune and Israel Regardie and other pioneers in the Western Mystery Tradition were practical journeymen seeing what worked to their own satisfaction, content to let the theory follow after.

This was by no means the same as mysticism, even though the term mysticism was often loosely applied to occultism. The mystic's aim was a direct relationship with God, whilst the role of the occultist was to explore, albeit with due responsibility and reverence, the inner aspects of God's creation. To be more precise in the use of terms, one form of experience and endeavour was *mystical*, the other type was *magical*. In this respect, it might have been more appropriate to call Dion Fortune's book the *Magical* rather than *The Mystical Qabalah*, even at risk of this term being confused with conjuring tricks or sensational novels.

But Tony Duncan's purpose in *The Christ, Psychotherapy and Magic* was not the conversion of occultists to the Christian faith but the presentation to Christians of what he saw as an almost unknown, greatly misunderstood and very enlightening philosophy. And it was in light of this intention that I arranged for it to be published by a well known general publisher, Allen & Unwin.

It was welcomed in the national press by the *Guardian* which proclaimed *"Now at least one clergyman has got the point and in this book urges his fellow Christians not to dismiss occultism either as a cranky fad or as a black art."* And as *"a wholly fascinating book which should be required reading for all church people."*

The gist of what he had to say to his fellow clergy was admirably contained in an article he wrote at this time for the theological journal *New Fire*.

THE REDISCOVERY OF TECHNIQUES

There is currently, on the fringes of the Church, but also in places more obviously within her community, a considerable movement apparent in matters spiritual. This movement is twofold and represents on the one hand a considerable re-awakening of interest in things of an interior and spiritual nature, and on the other, a clear revival of the long-forgotten and neglected eschatological hope. There is a "meditation movement" much in evidence and growing fast. There is also what may be described as a "New Age" movement which looks forward to a new order in things, which tends to express itself in astrological terms rather than theological, but which is for all that quite clearly eschatological in character. These two movements are part of a single whole.

The late C.G.Jung commented upon the obsession of modern man with the contents of his own subconscious. There is, in this shrinking world, small opportunity for high adventure left for the average man, and it may be this very fact which is beginning to move men and women to undertake voyages of discovery of an interior nature, seeking to penetrate the limitlessness "within" and arrive at some ultimate destination. The widespread experimentation with drugs is possibly a symptom of this sense of calling. Certainly the pantheistic experience of drug-taking is in tune with growing meditation and "new age" movements.

Modern Western man has rediscovered three very old and rather obvious truths:

1. The reality of the psychically perceived "inner dimension" of creation.
2. The possibility of conscious participation in this psychically perceived inner dimension. The growing interest in the occult is evidence of this, and the interest is growing and deepening.
3. That meditational techniques, commonplace in the East but neglected in the over-intellectualised West, provide a well-tried and effective means of penetrating the threshold of consciousness in a controlled manner without recourse to drugs.

There appears to be, in the rising generation, a considerable increase in what we may describe as "psychical awareness". In addition, there is a very real and growing desire for God. There is, however, a massive impatience with institutionalism, and a real questioning as to the relevance of the institutional Church to things of the spirit at all. Our public preoccupation with "relevance" and self-preservation has not helped us, but far worse has been the long tradition of ignorance in matters of an interior nature, our mistrust of mysticism and our rejection without very much attempt at comprehension of the "psychic". The movements I have mentioned are essentially lay movements, there is a dearth of theologically trained minds available to them, and a clergyman, to most people involved, is the very last person from whom they would expect to receive comprehension, let alone help and guidance! The situation is grotesque, but these are the facts.

Stated simply, what has been happening is a rediscovery of the human faculty of *intuitive knowledge*. Now there are three ways of "knowing"; the first way, which contains the others, is the way of Love. As the writer of the *Cloud of Unknowing* tells us, God may be known by loving but not by thinking: "by love may he be gotten and holden, but by thinking, never." The knowing of Love is the archetype of all knowing, and two *ways* of knowing depend upon it; the rational and intuitive. The first of these, the way of Reason, is the way of theology which is the rational expression of the revelations of divine Love. The second way of knowing is the way of Intuition, and this way has many different levels, and it may be said that there is the intuition of Grace and the intuition of Nature. But Reason and Intuition must be held in balance, for each is deformed without the other. The dreadful aridity and deformity of some Western Protestant theology exhibits vividly the effects of the kind of imbalance towards Reason only, to which the West has long been prone.

What is in progress is a rediscovery of balance by the development and stimulation of the intuition. This is necessary if man is to be fully human, and I believe that the movements described are of the Spirit. But where balance has been long deranged, the restoration thereof is likely to manifest imbalances, here and there, in the opposite direction. This is occasionally the case at the present time.

We have spoken of a meditation movement which is widespread and growing. Its tutors tend to be trained not in Western Christian techniques but in oriental methods. Yoga, Sufism, Buddhist and Hindu methods mix together with the not dissimilar methods of Western occultism. In the West, the neglected and misunderstood Rudolf Steiner is a source of inspiration and instruction for many. The great Christian heritage of mysticism and contemplation is going by default through sheer ignorance of it, and through the widespread gap in communication between those seeking God in meditation and those able to help them within the institutional Church, the clergy in particular.

The effects of this communications failure are dolorous. The terminologies are in hopeless confusion and the distinction between meditation as a *technique* and "meditation" when what is meant is "contemplation" is quite blurred. Meditators seek "Samadhi" and there is nobody to tell them that this is the same as "the Prayer of Union", and that the techniques employed, although potent, can only lead to the threshold of contemplation, and that technique is not the same thing as prayer. Furthermore, the techniques, because they are techniques only, can be used for many purposes. They can be used prayerfully, they can be used to simply induce an inner peace or silence without conscious desire to pray; and they can also be used to explore the unconscious mind, and this is not the same thing at all as prayer, although many practitioners of the occult think that it is.

Perhaps the most serious result of the failure, so far, in communication between the theologically trained minds of the institutional Church and the meditation movement within its ranks and upon its fringes is that the "occult" is regarded, both by the Church and by occult practitioners, as an "ism" rather than as an "ology". The growing awareness of the interior nuts and bolts of creation, of the psychic structure of man – a commonplace in oriental spirituality – is becoming a theology in its own right, and a monist one at that. For lack of dialogue, God is being identified with his creation and "psychic-nuts-and-boltsism" is tending to become a counterfeit religion. The fact that the Church has for so long forgotten, or discounted, that which has been commonplace to her natural psychics has tended to drive esotericism into dark corners rather than illuminate it with the Light of Christ. Nature has been damned in the name of Grace rather than perfected and transformed by it!

The Church has much to rediscover. The psychologically potent, and psychically informed techniques of meditation which are enshrined in the oriental disciplines can, on their own, only go so far. They belong to the dispensation of Nature, not of Grace. Many of the trials and tribulations suffered by those who seek to practice contemplative prayer in the West are caused by the sheer ignorance of Nature in this respect; and Grace works upon Nature, not in isolation from it. The marriage of the oriental techniques widely used in the meditation movement with the Christian mystical tradition is in process of haphazard celebration, but dialogue and a compassionate readiness to listen, to learn, and to theologically inform are, I believe, essential if a very great movement of the Spirit is to reach its proper fruition.

The movements I have outlined represent many strands of the one "rope". The meditation movement with its oriental methods, the new age movement with its awakening eschatological hope, the intuitive awakening and rediscovery of the inner dimensions of creation and the rediscovery and application to prayer of the psychic structure of man represent a movement of the Spirit of the greatest importance. As may be expected, a freakish "fringe" is much in evidence and makes much noise. There is a shadow side to the movement which manifests as witchcraft, occult dabbling and, occasionally, black magic. But it were the greatest folly, I submit, to identify the movement as a whole with its shadow; and it would be unfaithful and unloving indeed to rest in comfort within our Gothic institutions and close our eyes to what the Spirit is currently saying clearly, and excitingly, to the Churches.

A. D. DUNCAN

Much of this can be summed up in two poems of his, obviously written from experience, on the well-intentioned activity of a local meditation group and a more direct approach to divine source.

THE MEDITATION GROUP

We slip too simply into psychic silence
in technical accomplishment and group rapport.
The triggers touched are well prepared and primed,
all autonomic systems are at "go." One leads.

The target of each heart is to the rest unknown
but all are launched into their timeless hour
presuming common purpose. One dreams, one prays,
others are rapt in meditation. One manipulates.

The group unconscious, thus invoked, facilitates;
great works are done, phenomena abound;
a cosy glow pervades when all touch ground.

The tea is drunk, the notes exchanged
and all depart. Two headaches, one feels drained,
and one would have his great unease explained.

BALAAM'S DOG

The Lord, who made an ass articulate
in Holy Writ has, in these latter days
inspired my dog who, noticing my state
observed: "You seek our Lord in many ways;
You meditate for hours, breathe Yoga breath,
contort yourself in postures and awake
your inner depths to nightmare and near-death,
perform the *Dhikr*, and contemplate, and make
an inner Tantric sound; and go to bed
exhausted and tormented in the dark.
You make of Love such heavy work!" she said.
"With all these arrows, do you hit the mark?
Our Lord is here," she said. "Can you not see?
Our Lord is Love, and loving. Just like me!"

4

HIGHNAM

AT THE beginning of 1970, immediately after the publication of *The Christ, Psychotherapy & Magic*, Tony Duncan was moved on from Parkend to become Vicar of Highnam with Lassington and Rudford, a group of villages just to the northwest of Gloucester. Not long after, I too moved, over to Braintree in Essex to become an executive in a large educational publishing company.

The church at Highnam had a strange and sad history. A sadness that still seemed to hang over the place. It had been built by a Victorian philanthropist, artist and collector, Thomas Gambier Parry, famous for the development of the Gambier Parry process of fresco painting which adorns the cathedrals of Ely and Gloucester. Having become squire at Highnam Court in his early twenties he settled in with his wife Isabella, only to lose her and their three youngest children to tuberculosis.

A year after their death, in 1849, he began to build this vast church designed in Victorian Gothic style and dedicated to the Holy Innocents, and what was virtually a shrine and memorial for his lost loved ones. Completing it structurally within two years, he then began to cover its interior with frescoes using the technique he had invented himself. The wall paintings, which took him over 20 years to complete, were his own work and design, including grinding pigments from his own formula of beeswax, turpentine, spike lavender and assorted organic resins. They featured biblical quotations, many on themes of

Isabella Gambier Parry

·56·

judgement and redemption, with vines, blossoms and golden fleur de lys twirling up the arches and columns and passion flowers across the end walls. Over one of the aisles was a long frieze of biblical figures, and the chancel was covered with stars and angels. A side chapel, which also served as his private pew, was dedicated to his beloved Isabella, a bust of whom still stands in the niche where he placed it.

As every window was of stained glass, this great and glorious private sepulchre was quite a dark place under natural light, but in his day had been lit with many candles which in the early twentieth century were replaced by oil lamps. Unfortunately both candles and oil lamps give off large quantities of soot, and so over the years the beautiful paintings were covered with a patina of oily grime, and passed through dull grey almost to black. And because of the building's great size it became impossible to keep it in good repair. Parts began to crumble, rain came through the roof, and any damage was patched up as cheaply as possible. This was the state of affairs when Tony Duncan arrived, as he records in a poem about the place.

Highnam
[Church of the Holy Innocents]

The plaster cracks and drops, the frescoes fade;
the builder's cheats let water in, let fall
the ill-plugged pinnacles. A sinking floor
makes crazy the great candlesticks. Great books
of Cranmer's, bound in brass, now lie
dust-gathering, his Church has passed them by.

These holy innocents were carried off;
their Herod was tubercular, their mother's too.
This holy shrine is God's and theirs,
cemented by the Squire's cruel tears;
dark, lofty, mystic, beautiful and sad,
and crumbling, maturing, changing down the years.

The brick-box multitudes attend here now,
all brash and cheerful; their liturgy profound
but language vulgar, angular and new.
God's Holy Mother occupies the pew
where Squire glared and counted through the grille.
But I have seen, have seen! Unbound
and unbereaved, and out of time, and how
that older, gentler family attends here still.

It should be said that the "vulgar language" was not an aspersion on the culture of the modern congregation, but rather on current attempts to modernise the Anglican liturgy, and the Duncans were later very happy to join the multitudes, in a brick-box vicarage with central heating, as a blessed relief from the large cold damp Victorian pile.

As I recall from visiting the place, the church had an atmosphere of great sadness that was partly the result of signs of neglect – the sinking floor, the leaking pinnacles, the cracking plaster – nonetheless, as hinted in the last lines of his poem, there was somehow detectable under all this an underlying presence of a spirit of love.

In fact I felt this worth comment in a postscript to a letter I wrote him shortly after a visit in April 1971. "*P.S. I was much moved by Isabella on our visit to the church. It seems to me she's still around – but not in any pathological way.*"

To which, somewhat to my surprise, he replied: "*I entirely agree with you about Isabella – there is a story there too, but that was last year; she is still about and in the nicest way. She gave me a little 'talking to' the other day, which was very apropos and well received!*"

As to the story about her, he never revealed more, but I fancy it lies behind another poem he wrote:

Fierce Prayers

I soak up sadness of a piteous past
as if I were a sponge. The vinegar upon the hyssop stick
had tasted thus; and set about my shoulders
and my heavy head, the burden of it all.

And all to set before the Living Lord,
invoke the saving Mysteries of one true Faith
and pray fierce prayers. Beneath, beneath it all
the human tragedy, the broken human heart.

What's time within the context of Eternity?
What prim parameters shall tightly limit Love?
What use the human heart if not to break
one for another, or the hands if not to hold?
The myriad persons of one Creature, we;
what's warmth if Love will see another cold?

He was, at this time, did we but know it, on the threshold of a remarkable change of perspective through attending a conference at Iona a month later – just as Highnam church itself was destined for major change in later years with a resurrection of its former glories. Tom Fenton, a great-grandson of the founder, inherited the estate in the early 1970s and from 1987 to 1994 began a fund-raising campaign to fix the roof and clean the frescoes. These were finally revealed in all their pristine

The restored frescoes in Highnam church

beauty, to the point that the church today has become a mid-Victorian attraction for coach parties to visit, with the added interest that one of Thomas Gambier Parry's surviving children became the celebrated musician who composed, amongst other church music, the setting for William Blake's *Jerusalem*.

All this restoration came after Tony Duncan's time, although he did eventually see it all in its original glory on a visit back to Gloucestershire in 2001.

> We have just returned from Gloucestershire. We stayed three nights in Tewkesbury and went to the Abbey on Sunday morning, before going to Highnam, my second parish, for the 150th Anniversary of its Consecration. I was paraded as "a former Rector" which made me feel frightfully senior. Like the Abbey, which is doing, numerically, exactly twice as well as when we were there, so Highnam is in great heart with all the Victorian murals restored spectacularly. We came home via Bristol and Cheshire, dropping in on friends. Perfect blue skies, countryside looking wonderful – and Helga took her rail of Fashion Clothes and gathered orders worth £1200! We could afford the petrol home!
>
> Heaven has a sense of humour, as well we know. When we were in Highnam we were nothing if not strapped for cash and Helga was making everything she wore. One had to keep up appearances, but...

It so happened that, on arrival for the Anniversary, I stepped out of a gleaming white Mercedes-Benz wearing a Gieves and Hawkes suit that cost £1000, topped by a Cheltenham overcoat complete with velvet collar! This perfect manifestation of clerical poverty was enabled by a) Helga's cousin who cheerfully flogged his then 15-year-old Merc to us for DM1000 (£350) three years ago; b) a friend in Corbridge whose deceased husband was exactly my size and fit who had 'lashed out' just before the dreaded diagnosis; c) a Hexham Charity Shop! Moral: Never judge by appearances!

However, to return to our original time line, the seeds of change were beginning to show, as revealed in a letter he wrote to me in January 1970 immediately after arriving at Highnam. He was in the gestation period of another book, *The Priesthood of Man*. His definition of a priest was one who stands at the intersection between two worlds, in whom two worlds meet, and who is the "door" between them. And that mankind was "God's priest to Creation", standing as mediator between God and the created order of things, leading to some challenging pronouncements on the human condition. Not least on our responsibility for the environment, and for the things and creatures that technology had placed more and more in our power.

He also acknowledged the validity of a very large *range* of priesthoods and a number of different "worlds". The idea of "functioning as a priest of the Old Religion" had once raised his hackles when he had seen it referring to an enthusiast of the burgeoning neo-pagan movement. But now he began to recognise that priesthoods of the old and new were not necessarily in opposition, did not compete, but were doors opening to different (but not necessarily opposed) worlds.

Indeed, towards the end of the year he wrote to tell me how an old friend and fellow cleric – who had the natural ability to astrally project but never used it as he felt it was wrong – had rooted him to the ground with a profound discussion on the relationship between the Church (as small, Eucharistic minority group) and the "old gods" (created good in themselves but redeemed in Christ). Far from being equated with demons, as Milton had averred in *Paradise Lost*, they were currently reinstating and stimulating the natural religion in man, and through whom the Holy Spirit could work through to the great mass of the community.

He realised this to be a very thought-provoking theory, the ramifications of which were endless and exciting. He was sure the stifling of religion with "churchianity" had left society high and dry spiritually. And what is more, that an over-institutionalised church was about to take a real toss for her soul's health!

In reply to some blistering remarks I had made about "clerical bureaucracy" he sought to reassure me that the Parochial System, "with its ball and chain 19th century Churchianity" was beginning to mutate – slowly in some places, but faster in others.

> I am not for abolishing it (*the Parochial system*) by any means, but it has "cornered the market" far too much since the Reformation. We are too institutionalised and the Institution as such is beginning to have the boot put in by the Almighty. I think stage one is a financial strangle to crack the hard shell; after that, anything can happen and I find this an exciting time to live and work in.
>
> One has to re-distil one's motives all the time, and I believe genuine creativity is wholly dependent upon integrity. And I am coming to think that Integrity is what matters most in any man.
>
> I must now bend my efforts to devise a "Bible Quiz" for the Women's Fellowship Beetle-Drive and Social this afternoon! Yes, I am serious! Thank God for a sense of humour.

(He also demonstrated a sense of humour by writing to me once or twice on letter headings of THE BISHOP OF WILLESDEN'S COMMISSION TO EXAMINE THE OBJECTS AND CONSIDER THE POLICY OF THE MOTHERS' UNION, to which he had been appointed.)

He had had some very interesting letters as a result of the publication of *The Christ, Psychotherapy & Magic,* all of them very appreciative he was happy to say. The reviews had been kind as well – apart from one theological journal which he said was emotional and obviously frightened. He had been told that the reviewer had been a friend of Charles Williams[2] and had met a great deal of very "Black" stuff in his time.

He found the times very exciting – if a bit alarming – and he had a strong feeling that "something was up" along with a great sense of urgency, particularly in the realm of ideas. He could not help thinking that there was a lot of overtime being worked on the "inner planes", and in heaven too!

---

2 An unconventional Christian mystic and Rosicrucian, one of the Inklings, and author (inter alia) of a series of occult novels featuring some of the dark side that could be associated with magic. For more detail see my *The Magical World of the Inklings* (Skylight Press).

The idea of "the Masters" (inner plane contacts whom I respected and with whom I worked) seemed very reasonable to him now. He had sorted out a lot of things and managed to get them more or less where they ought to be – at least to his own satisfaction. This included even reincarnation (*if I must!*) which he did not think was really at odds with the Christian doctrine of the Resurrection of the Body – that is to say, the whole man. But he was bored with the idea of coming back *again*. "Blow that, I want God!" was how he succinctly put it.

A few months later he wrote to say he had written more pages of *The Priesthood of Man* which he described as "a piece of 'way-out' theology with a deceptively trad style". He was getting very excited about the relationship between Heaven and Earth – and by "the Earth" meaning the *within* of the whole Cosmos, or what I would call the "inner planes".

The Old Testament, the Upanishads, the Buddhist scriptures, some of W.G. Gray's stuff and all kinds of things had helped, including Teilhard de Chardin, to establish the idea of the *within* of the Cosmos as a thing *other* than "Heaven". Underlying which was the realisation of the "priesthood of man" in its many aspects.

He intended to get on with this after Easter but his previous hunch about there being "something up" burst into fruition in May 1971 after taking part in a conference on the holy island of Iona. He wrote to me in high excitement immediately afterwards.

> The conference was utterly remarkable. The initiative was from a number of devout Christian laymen and women who were gifted healers, and some highly sensitive in terms of clairvoyance and clairaudience, mediums, etc. The lecturers included a Polish RC priest who is a mystic, a nuclear physicist, a sound theologian, a perpetual hyper-sensitive clairvoyant and a Saint of God! Full house!
>
> There was a Church of Scotland minister with experience in this field, and there was me. Also two ladies who read "letters" from certain of the departed (one was a very gifted medium – clairaudience, she told me all about it) and whereas I began listening with all red lights flashing, I am bound to say that they were rapidly extinguished, so self-authenticating were the "letters".[3]

---

[3] These were *Letters from our Daughters* by the novelist Rosamond Lehman and the gifted clairaudient Lady Cynthia Sandys, published as booklets by the College of Psychic Studies.

There were daily meditations, conducted by the chairman, a very gifted healer (my old regiment – must be OK!) which put the occult techniques firmly into a Christian context and made their efficiency and their relevance plain. Our little RC managed to unite the relationship of the Collective Unconscious with the Divine Life/nuclear physics/meditation technique/sheer holiness, to such a degree of simple, obvious lucidity that we all wondered why we had not seen it before. And of course we all had – but here was the reasoned expression of it.

I gave two lectures; the first was a theological framework (a precis of the book to date, with traces of the unwritten bit), and this went down very well I am glad to say. The second was an outline of the Qabala (precis of *our* book[4]) which a few folk knew a little about, and all were very interested. I gave a third talk, about bits and pieces of my ministry to the disturbed departed. By this time I had very clearly realised the extent to which constant ministry to sickness inhibits one's view of health. I am happy to say that this went down well too. But, for me, the Conference was one great session of learning and clarification. The next bit(s) of the book are in skeleton all over the place in my mind. I am exhilarated and at the same time horrified at the thought of the task. But it is clear that I am intended to get on with it!

There were 70 people there, including a Bishop, two titled ladies and a small sprinkling of very lovely hippies. (Lovely as people, not to look at!) The bond of charity which very quickly united us, the truly supernatural rapport, was itself as much in the way of "validating" the proceedings as anyone could wish for. And you would have been thrilled – as I hope you are at second hand – at the way in which the occult and the faith, and the insights of the mechanics of things, simply came together as, manifestly, parts of the one unity. The instincts that we have shared about this are in sight of fruition, and all of us in Iona were quite clear, I think, that things could never be the same again, that we were firmly set upon a new plane, and that it had been our privilege to be in on the beginning of an epoch.

More later, but I am writing in haste with diminished coherence. Firmly under Aquarius, and vibrating like nobody's business, I remain, Yours "Aye", Tony.

As an aftermath to all this, as he later wrote, he had had some "pretty staggering experiences" in which all kinds of things seemed to be happening – or were "threatening to happen in the nicest possible way."

---

4 *The Christ, Psychotherapy & Magic,* Allen & Unwin, 1969; Helios, 1975; Skylight Press, 2012.

He also said that the Devic world had made itself very noticeable since about July. He did not elaborate on this and the extent of it did not occur to me at the time, until I read an essay of his, written many years later and not published in his lifetime.

AWAY WITH THE FAIRIES

There are fairies at the bottom of my garden. To be truthful, I am uncertain as to the fairy population in the tiny garden of my present semi-detached villa, brick-built and bow-windowed in the best fashion of the 1930s. I have no doubt, however, that fairies abounded in the much bigger and much wider gardens of the various country Vicarages and Rectories which it has been my privilege to occupy over the years.

That the garden of Parkend Vicarage in the Forest of Dean was thickly populated I have no doubt whatever, but I was then insensitive to the plane upon which the fairy kingdoms operate. It was in the garden of Highnam Rectory that I entered into, not only an awareness of this segment of Earthly reality, but also a conscious, courteous – even affectionate – "modus vivendi" with my resident fairy population. I remember them most kindly; we had become friends.

For a period of some three or four years my range of perception was extended to include periodic encounters with the world of Faerie. This included other, Elemental spirits – entities, call them what you will – and this latter sensitivity to spirits of Earth, Air, Water and Fire was not always comfortable. Happily, and importantly, this extension of perception was a thing given and by no means sought. Looking back upon that period of my life I clearly recognise it as both appropriate to the time and purposeful in terms of my own becoming.

Gifts of extended perception are granted, I believe, on a "need to know" basis. I clearly had a need to know and, above all, a need to have compassion and understanding for that which I was encountering. To encounter with the head only is to fall into delusions of "esoteric knowledge" with all its ego inflating and corrupting possibilities.

To encounter with both heart and mind is to be open to the learning of compassion and understanding. Affection and respect are two constituents of love, without which encounters with the worlds of Elementals and of Faerie can fast degenerate into exercises in manipulative magic.

The extension of my perception into the world of Faerie had another purpose, as I now understand it. I was to learn a measure of humility.

Humility has been aptly described as the acceptance of Reality, a thing very difficult for mortal men and women. In this case the lesson in humility involved me in abandoning for good any last trace of that rationalistic arrogance which will not accept anything other than itself and which denies all possibility of existence to other creatures on other levels or planes of being.

To be truthful, I had never had serious difficulties in accepting the possibility of Faerie, but now was obliged to face this part of reality fairly and squarely and take it into both my mind and my heart. I then had to learn to mind my own business all over again, for Faerie is its own business, not mine.

A further dimension of humility that I was now obliged to learn was the clear sight and understanding of that most unfaithful folly of all for any Christian man or woman: the arbitrary consigning of the whole intuitive and perceptive realm to darkness, as if it were exclusively the province of "the devil and his angels."

This is rationalistic arrogance gone mad, decked out with all the trappings of religiosity. Its underlying dynamic is not Faith but fear, and fear is the denial of love and of the reality of the love of God.

The consignment of the human intuitive faculty to the realms of darkness adds up to a fifty-per-cent denial of the Incarnation!

The world of Faery did me a great service. I learned, fairly quickly, that affection and respect breach great walls of mutual apprehension and uncertainty. Having learned this I then discovered that affection and respect are mutually generating. Having made this discovery the world of Faerie faded from my field of perception and has never returned to it. But I acknowledge its reality and its presence all around me. I shall not forget it.

He also wrote a poem along these lines.

The Friendship of Faerie

Shall I return to fairyland
who saw them dancing there?
Shall I return and part the veil
that hangs across thin air?
Shall I intrude upon their peace
who once did welcome me?
Or might our blessed friendship cease
should I, intruding, see?

True magic is a given thing,
its mysteries are not sought;
its unexpected light and love
not stolen are, nor bought.
An open heart, a true respect
for brethren yet unseen
shall yield what no man can expect
who comes where Love has been.

However, something rather more startling was to come my way from him early next year, in 1972, in the form of a manuscript called *The Lord of the Dance*. This was no cautious intellectual analysis like *The Christ, Psychotherapy & Magic* nor a theological exposition like *Pray & Live* or *The Whole Christ*, but a straight "in your face" mystical contact.

It began with a vision of the created universe as a great dance:

> The whole creation is dancing; the whole universe – galaxies, nebulae, stars and their satellites – is engaged in the Great Dance. They turn, and come together, and draw apart, and come together again. And so it has ever been, and so it shall ever be through all eternity. Creation makes its own music. There is no created being that does not sing, and the music of everything that is joins together to make the great Harmony and Rhythm of the Dance.

and it ended with a direct call from its Creator, the Lord of the Dance:

> Oh Earth! Rejoice, for your sorrow is ended.
> Now shall your beauty be made manifest.
> Sing, O Earth! See: I dance to your music.
> You shall sing at my Wedding.
> Now is the Moment of Truth;
> now, behold, I AM.

He sent it off to Allen & Unwin who as rapidly batted it back to him, as I could have foretold. As I saw it, there was no chance any commercial publisher was going to take this on. The book seemed to me to be years ahead of its time and at any rate I found it deeply inspiring. I suggested that rather than spend time hawking it round to publishers, knocking in vain from inn door to inn door, he bring the little waif to birth in my humble stable. In other words, have it published by Helios.

I was a little concerned about whether he might find it professionally compromising to have his name on a Helios book and suggested he might think about using a pseudonym – "Brother Herbert" I suggested, somewhat jocularly. As I suspected he responded quite firmly:

> As to "Brother Herbert" – Helga's hoots of derision could be heard in advance – and would be deserved. No, let us not dissemble or cloak things. I can't quite trust pen-names. (No disrespect to G.K. – I mean my own inclinations in this direction.) And if I am to be under a professional cloud, it will be nothing to the cloud I am likely to be under after Saturday's Synod when I tell our Bishop what I think of his theology apropos of Anglican-Methodist "something-or-other"!

And indeed something which I might have expected, bearing in mind a quotation from his manuscript:

> "O Man! Will you be fearful? Will you hedge yourself about with law? I will teach you to be free with that freedom I won for you. I do not want you law-abiding. I want you as you are. I do not will compliance; I require integrity."

Obviously Tony Duncan believed in practising what he preached! And so this remarkable book appeared, just six months later, in November 1972.

His own view was, the more he thought about it, that Helios was the right and proper publisher for it. He could not think what the *Church Times* might say but reckoned that in five years time the paper would either be dead or different. Or as he put it "the whole field of theological writing is suffering from fallen arches and ingrowing toenails. Or its chosen feet made of clay – barren intellectualism, dried out!"

His views on this situation were aptly summed up in another little poem of his, somewhat idiosyncratically entitled *Witchcraft* although the witches he had in mind were dry as dust intellectuals.

Witchcraft

The group-unconscious witchcrafts of the world
manipulate perception and make blind.
An intellectual ambience, like poison gas,
pervades to paralyse, and through its choking swirls
I fumble for my respirator, cling to Faith.

This clever world of two dimensions
and rationalist religion is a living death.
I burst, uncouth, a monster, from its room,
breathe sweet fresh air through all its cracks
and rise, regenerate, from out the splintered tomb

As for the prospects for the *The Lord of the Dance*, he thought it likely to attract or repel equally on both sides of the Church. Some ultra-prots would not hear of anything they had not written themselves, and a few remaining "more Catholic than the Pope" Anglicans would not like it either. As for the rest – the field was wide open or tight shut fairly equally.

It caused no immediate revolution in church or state but was and is a book I was proud to publish. But it was hardly off the presses before he followed up with another manuscript of a remarkable nature. *The Sword in the Sun* was in the form of a dialogue with an angel, with occasional interjections from an Elemental hierarch!

As well as being an instructive book, it was a very self revelatory one as well, for it was illustrated at key points with poems written by himself, on the grounds that a poem could express things that could not be said in any other way. He found himself drawing out from some of them things that he had not realised in the writing of them. One example being:

I Cried Aloud

I cried aloud; a wild and bitter cry.
Bats fluttered from the eaves, a window lit,
a murmuring of voices stirred and stilled.
I lay in horror, staring at the sky.

Full seven years past I passed that way;
the house has gone now, in its place
a bypass thunders. There remains no trace
nor shade, nor memory today.

So time and place and people move apart
and fashions change, and seasons turn,
and time and times run on. Beneath it all
eternity lies constant. All who rise (or fall)
and face that searing darkness, burn.
I bear the scar forever on my heart.

About which the angel says:

ANGEL: It was yourself you were fighting, and you thought it was the devil! You bear the scars yet, but they are healed.

ME: Self or the devil, it is hard to tell one from another sometimes.

ANGEL: Too long you were identified.

ME: What do you mean? Before this present life? Before the Incarnation?

ANGEL: Both; but no matter now. That battle has been won.

Deep matters here – rather beyond the conventional beliefs of Anthony Duncan as Anglican vicar – implying reincarnation, and that going long back to pre-Christian times.
   He was asked "to sing again" of his past mystical experience, experienced and written when he was at theological college.

HE CAME, AS HE SAID...

He came, as he said, a thief in the night;
as a darkness darker than the darkness;
unheard, unexpected, unprepared for.

Time tarried but a breath, a parting of the lips,
an opening of the eyes wide; closing, infolding
on that which pierced their lids and possessed.
Time tarried but a stirring of the hand,
a laying wide, a closing and infolding

on that which pierced the naked soul
and possessed.

O Darkness, Darkness;
                      Holy and Mighty.

He came, a darkness; clad in the smoke
of holy fire. He came as the North and
as the South Wind, breathed upon
his moonlit garden, and the spices flowed;
the precious fruits were tasted, and found rest.

O Darkness, Darkness;
                      Holy and Mighty.

The daughters of Jerusalem, the roes and hinds
of the scented fields, stirred not up
nor wakened;
but Time from his tall tower called:
Time, time, time:
It is not time,
submit to time,
be a wall of time,
a door of time;
there is yet time.

O Darkness, Darkness;
                      Holy and Mighty.
    Holy, Immortal:
                      Return.

ANGEL: What was this of which you were singing? Do you know?

ME: I hardly know. It was a terrible embrace; a ravishing. I know no other word for it. And I was sad indeed when it was past. Interpret it for me, my Brother, if you will.

ANGEL: A ravishing it was indeed! But that word has an unhappy meaning for mortal men, and this was Joy eternal. Others have sung of the same love-making.

ME: Yes, others whose names I dare not utter in the same breath as my own for mortal terror of presumption.

ANGEL: You will hang on to hierarchies. Your Lord loves the lowest dog-thief as dearly as he loves you. And does he love "heroic saints" the more? This does not make you perfect, little Brother. Your consciousness has undergone some evolution in the dimension of prayer; it is a moral evolution, but it does not leave you faultless as your wife and children will be quick to tell you. And should you like me to remind you of a failing or two for fear you should imagine yourself a "Saint?"

ME: I don't think I believe in "Saints" as once I did. I think it safe for you to forego the sorrow of such dolorous reminders. I am not likely to forget my failings; they will not let me!

ANGEL: Men do not wind themselves aloft in prayer. You have written yourself that prayer is a matter of the will. So it is. And those who think only of "raising consciousness" are sailing close to magic. Nevertheless, in prayer, consciousness may indeed by raised, and in prayer this is no longer magic – it is mysticism. The two could not be further apart.

However, all was not on this deep moral and theological level but called into being some insights into what might be called the "Divine Identification" of God with the natural world. As in an evocation of one of the little parish churches he was responsible for at Highnam, at Rudford, which going back to Anglo-Saxon times, spoke of the *process* of things.

THE LITTLE CHURCH AND CHURCHYARD AT RUDFORD

Once upon Eternity, under a changing sky
when shadows moved, stirring the stillness of a stream
slow, slowly out of time; once, once where ley
lines swung upon a dance, and passing spirits passed
from time, through timelessness, to time again;
once, here, the rough stones squared the ring
and set the cross upon a crossing of the way,
and nailed a blessing to this spot for me.

Highnam

Now, at the grey time of the river's rising,
while spirits wait on trembling wing,
the long-dead whisper at the great oak door.
The waters of the wise wake, swirl and splash
in their stone-set sea, and the grey stones sing;
rooks rise to the heavens and race in a ring
to a changing sky from all change free
Nobis quoque peccatoribus – Eternity!

Once upon Eternity *"when the Clerkes have dooen singing,*
To saue and defend thy seruant our Kyng,"
thy Angel over the wide waste winging
a stillness animate – shall shatter with light
the stream, the stones, the dance and the ring,
the changing sky and the great door's might,
time, the long-dead, timelessness and me;
redeem all, once, for all Eternity.

Church of St Mary the Virgin, Rudford

Or returning to memories of the Forest of Dean at Parkend and the realisation of the Love in all things:

ETERNITY

I sat upon a fallen tree,
and looked and saw Eternity.
The lovers thronged upon the road
and passed and passed; are passing still,
their feet a whisper in the grass;
their voice a wind upon the hill.

And as I sat and lingered there,
they met, and filled the shining air
'til suddenly – all things were new!
And tree and leaf, and earth and stone,
and running water woke, and sang.
All sang for joy – save me alone.

I rose up from that fallen tree
and took my quest – Eternity!
I'll search the caverns of the moon
and climb the high hills of the sun
till love and lovers fill the sky;
and they, the elements and I are one.

Or as in the first line of the third stanza of the poem that follows *"Here the Word looks through created eyes"*, the Angel is moved to say *"That was well said. That is your priesthood, little Brother; it is the priesthood of man."*

OAKENHILL WOOD

Now is a slow, unfolding moment
Perpetually present. Here is always now.
Time passed with the track's end,
And my stride shortened, and slowed, and stilled,
And stopped, soft-carpeted in deep silence.

Highnam

Here is a universe of tall trees:
Trunk after trunk to the world's end,
Numberless, endless, silent.
And here my consciousness, here my priesthood
Sees, and loves, and animates.

Here the Word looks through created eyes
Adoring in creation the Creator. Here
Is Love; and now, the Trinity.

However, the time came in this same year, 1972, when, perhaps as a consequence of the arrival of Tom Fenton, the great-grandson of the founder, inheriting the estate, the Duncans found themselves freed from the ancient vicarage in favour of a less pretentious abode on a local housing estate, with the modern blessing of central heating.

This brought about an appraisal in light verse of some of the neighbours and parishioners, as Tony Duncan found himself in closer proximity to their workaday lives.

Red Bricks in the Grey of Dawn

Awake betimes I greet the dawn;
our early breakfast-time prepare
in peace, providing time and space
for wifely Yoga, Face and Hair.

And all about our small estate
the worlds therein begin to stir;
while half-attending to my tasks
I note what daily doth occur.

A cat from out his cat-flap flips,
wipes dainty mouth with velvet paw,
then lightly leaps the fence between
for second breakfast set next door.

Dog Sam beneath the table sits,
with whiskers raised to realms above,
and heavenward howls the heartbreak songs
of unrequited doggy love.

The garage lad with turbo car
slams on the stereo, grinds the gear,
then backs full-throttle down the lane
with bongos banging in his ear.

Across the Green, the curtains closed
pull promptly open in the bay
and, crisp as clockwork, both depart:
he in a red car, she in grey.

With diesel-engined clatter-bang
one house awakens with a roar;
subsides in silence and in sleep
at clash and clang of garage door.

The paper-lad, with yellow bag,
walks weary round, his pittance waits.
He shoves the papers through their slots
and scuffs his trainers, clangs the gates.

Jam-sandwich-painted sit the cars
that night and day patrol our peace.
In short-wave silence steam the cups;
the kettle's on for the Police

Along with a certain amount of somewhat conservative comment on the lifestyles of one or two:

THE BONNY LASS

A bonny lass is yon. And bright,
with flair for fast promotion.
Was married, but it wasn't right
and ended in commotion.
He wanted kids, she her career;
the thing was dead within a year.
Divorced, she felt much better;
no strings, no row,
he's married now,
but still he can't forget her.

A bonny lass. She's done all right;
a company director.
Nice house, nice car: she's sitting tight,
needs no one to protect her.
She dresses well, the looking-glass
is kind about the years that pass
and men find her attractive.
Strings them along,
but not for long:
just casual, keeping active.

A bonny lass, with lots of friends,
all women with careers.
Her holidays abroad she spends
and seems to have no fears
for future and what it might hold,
what life's about, or growing old;
needs of the moment meeting.
Her current boy?
So young! A toy!
Like sweets for comfort eating!

And a certain confession of personal peccadilloes rather closer to home,
although this may well have been from Parkend.

Conspiracy

The Doctor, the Dentist and the Vicar fled
in darkness before dawn, the roads all black with ice,
a bitter chill pervading. The village was asleep;
cats on garden walls the only watch did keep.

The nurse would make appointments for another day,
the Doctor's headlights flashed along the deep
dark hedgerows. The three men, silent, tense
with earnest, expectation, hurried hence.

A Chapter Meeting, open-eyed forgot,
pin-pricked a Priest impatient with pretence.
He shrugged it off and grunted, first he'd missed for years;
they skidded on an icy patch and grappled with the gears.

They sped on East for Oxford with the Cotswolds grey,
reluctant dawning, mindful of the fears
that freezing fog frustrate what lay ahead.
Three truants, each as if a price upon his head.

Conspiracy was this! A secret setting off,
a conscious naughtiness, whatever might be said.
They got the length of London; gave three cheers
for the Annual Exhibition of Model Engineers!

Meanwhile, the typescript of *The Priesthood of Man* had been batting to and fro between us in typescript form and was accepted by the publishers Geoffrey Bles. So he now sent them *The Sword in the Sun*.

I was somewhat concerned about this, particularly in regard to his professional reputation, and wrote to warn him.

> I have now had time to read through *The Sword in the Sun* carefully a second time. This rather confirms what I said first time. This is, that if it appears under your own name it will not do a lot of good to anyone and least of all to yourself. What is more it could well destroy your credibility and thus cause the good influence of your previous books to come to nothing. There was a slight risk of this in *The Lord of the Dance* but an acceptable one. With the new one I think the risk would be wholly unacceptable.
>
> A rather subtle problem of integrity is involved I think. I'm sure I don't have to spell it out for you, but I'm sure that we don't want martyrdom – on the simple grounds that it would be counter-productive.
>
> After a pause to see how *The Lord of the Dance* goes, and the various hares it sets going, I would see it as possibly being published by Helios with anonymous authorship, called *Conversations with an Angel* or something similar. There is a lot in the book that will help to redeem much of occultism onto a Christocentric basis. I am sure it will be quite useless, and even detrimental, to orthodox church people. What esoteric truths it contains will be incomprehensible – and where comprehensible, alienating.
>
> Of course it would also be OK I think if Bles published it with the anonymous proviso.

He wrote back with typical deep thought, courage and integrity.

Many thanks for the letter. Yes, you have made explicit every single reservation I have about *The Sword in the Sun* and I don't dispute a word of what you say.

I find myself faced with a pretty problem – that of "stewardship" of what has been given. With <u>everything</u> since *The Christ, Psychotherapy & Magic* there has been this sense of growing vulnerability, of impending disaster in terms of what people will think. I felt it strongly about *The Lord of the Dance* and feel it strongly about *Priesthood of Man* too. In terms of worldly advancement in the institutional Church, one feels "a bad risk!" But <u>timing</u> is the important thing. I believe that I have to be prepared to be totally vulnerable in order to preserve the integrity of things. After being so prepared, then it may be that other, less alarming things may happen.

I doubt if Bles will take *Sword in the Sun*. They have signed up and paid advance of royalties – and their list is "broad-minded" so no doubt they will go through with *Priesthood of Man*. Such lights as I have indicated "wait and see!" Who knows, it may have to wait a long time, and be a "source" for other things as you suggest until the time is ripe. I just don't know. But as my vocation includes being a "bridge" between the institutional Church and the esoteric "fringes", and as this is, as you say, a "keystone" in the arch we have found ourselves building, I am bound to be confident (by faith if not by feeling!) that its time, place and manner of appearance will be given as surely as its text. In the meantime I have to be torn in two between excitement at it and horror at all the ghastly possible implications (sentimentality and self-advertisement being, for me, the worst). Apropos of the "bridge" vocation, I doubt if "they" will be so ham-fisted as to demolish the piers by dropping the span heavily and prematurely upon them! But there again, there may be method in such madness.

I propose to wait and see. I can do nothing else. If Bles say no (which I half hope they will) then the right answer will appear. If they say yes – well that might be the right answer. But it might be nice if the thing were "discovered" posthumously! That way I need not worry one way or the other. Trouble is, one has to arrange to be posthumous!

Yes, *Sword in the Sun* is a bit of a powder keg. All the "guidance" I get is a broad grin and "wait and see!" And that is what I must do – until Bles say something (even if it <u>is</u> "aaaagh!"). Then will be the time for decision and I am confident that the right answer will come. Till then – cliff hanging and much "oo-er!" But don't underestimate the great weight – far more than I think you realise – of real "trad" Christian mystical and theological tradition in *Sword in the Sun*. It is not more "way out" in fact than *Priesthood of Man* or *Lord of the Dance*. But it is "way out" in style and presentation to an alarming degree (for me), and the real horror, for my money, is the danger of self-advertisement and sentimentality. Anonymous, posthumous I should prefer! But we must wait and see! One thing is morally certain – there must be (or have been) the willingness to accept rejection, martyrdom etc., etc., for truth's sake. This is done in the sending it, in my own name, to a publisher. After this the way is clear for the real future of the work to be given. So I am not worried a bit – just terrified, that's all!

However, we did not have to wait too long, for the angel seemed to take the initiative, and come knocking on my door, so to speak. Not in any vision but in strong intuitive pressure, to put it to me in no uncertain terms that I should get down to writing a new textbook, as a follow up, and to a certain degree a corrective, to some of the assumptions in *A Practical Guide to Qabalistic Symbolism*. This was the beginnings of my book, *Experience of the Inner Worlds* published a couple of years later, its ten chapters and accompanying exercises based on key phrases in *The Lord of the Dance* and *The Sword in the Sun*.

Bles duly returned *The Sword in the Sun*, probably unread owing to some staffing difficulties they were having in the office, but confirming their commitment to *The Priesthood of Man*. Their commissioning editor even wrote to say "I continue to tell many people about *The Lord of the Dance* which I think is an astonishing piece of work."

But physical changes were also on the way. Tony Duncan wrote to me at the end of November 1972 to say "The Almighty is beginning to 'show his hand'. I have known something is up but have not known what. I think the New Year will have some surprises in store... I think I now know what to do about *The Sword in the Sun* – nothing! Sending it to a publisher was an act of faith. Now I must hang on to it, use it as a 'mine' and let its time-fuse tick away in the cellar!"

In fact *The Sword in the Sun* ticked away in the cellar for another twenty-five years before it appeared, and then in a far country, when a member of my group, Coleston Brown, set about publishing a whole series of books by both of us through his Sun Chalice imprint in the United States of America.

The immediate surprise in store turned out to be a shift of location for Tony Duncan, from rural Gloucestershire to an inner city church in the industrial north at Newcastle upon Tyne. A very different milieu from the past and present.

Hawkwood College, near Stroud, Gloucestershire

The move was due in May 1973, but immediately before that something of a date with destiny occurred. He was asked by the Gloucester Diocese to give a weekend of lectures at Hawkwood, a private college for adults founded on principles inspired by the esoteric teacher on "spiritual science" Rudolf Steiner, where a wide range of people were invited to run their own courses, seminars and conferences.

The subject he chose was *The Two Qabalahs,* and his talks largely a résumé of *The Christ, Psychotherapy & Magic* to show that there was some difference between the Qabalah as a direct approach to God or as a ground plan of the "inner planes" (what he liked to call "the psychic nuts and bolts of Creation"). In short, the difference, largely unperceived, between mysticism ad occultism.

In the event the talks went very well, and Tony Duncan reckoned it was the best audience he had spoken to for a very long time. There was however an awkward squad present who did not take all kindly to a clergyman making the slightest criticism of *A Practical Guide to Qabalistic Symbolism* (which they regarded something like holy writ) and felt betrayed when I stood up to agree with him.

The irony was that they were members of the *Helios Course on the Practical Qabalah* which I had launched some ten years previously in conjunction with John & Mary Hall and W.E. Butler. And I realised that if I wanted to introduce any new ideas into esoteric teaching along the lines Tony Duncan and I had discussed over the past decade it needed to be through a completely new initiative. This no doubt the angel had had in mind in getting me started on a new book, *Experience of the Inner Worlds*, a few months before. So I began recruiting students for what was to become the Gareth Knight Group, hiving off the Helios course as a separate entity under the name of the Servants of the Light. (Which I must say, has enjoyed considerable success over the years under Dolores and Michael Ashcroft-Nowicki – the esoteric pond being quite big enough for different fish to thrive in it.)

In the immediate fallout from the 1973 event I published a booklet of Tony Duncan's lectures, under the title of *The Two Qabalahs*, from which two or three introductory paragraphs from the first lecture (*A Christian's Approach to the Esoteric*) are worth quoting.

> It is, I think, something of a commentary on the curious times in which we live that quite a lot of people will think it odd that a Christian Priest should be giving a course of lectures on Occultism. This hasn't anything to do with "the Church" they say. And others will possibly think that a respectable clergyman should not have anything to do with such an obviously shady subject. Dark mutterings of "Black Magic" may possibly be heard in corners, especially those in which ignorance both of the Faith and of the occult is almost total!
>
> The Western Church tended to inhibit the gifts of the Spirit by placing controls upon them which reflected the prevailing Western European temperament to save people from themselves and "do them good" thereby. From the 11th century onwards the Papacy entered a period of decline which reflected itself in a growing imbalance towards intellectualism, over-centralisation and a very worldly concept of the Western Church as a kind of spiritual Empire with the subjects doing as they were told. The esoteric is always fascinating, and its fascinations produced a number of morbid movements against which the Church began to react with a curiously secular form of violence. Before long, the esoteric in general was identified with morbidity – especially where lay people were concerned – and the time came when it was dangerous to be a psychic for fear of denunciations on grounds of witchcraft or heresy of some kind.
>
> The Western Church was less inhibited where the theologically trained clergy and religious were concerned…What is forbidden for laymen and women is respectable for certain clergy…This is, in a nut-shell, the high medieval, Western approach to the esoteric. It reflects a very deficient understanding of what the Church is, in that it arbitrarily separates clergy

> and laity from each other and tends to identify "the Church" with its clerical hierarchy. This was, in fact, the great error of the Western Church. ... It is only now beginning to be realised that the laity have as much right, and indeed as much need to be competent in theology as the clergy. Universal education has not only saved us from medieval concepts of hierarchy, it demands of the Church that she attend more seriously to the fullness of her own humanity. This involved the Church, both clergy and laity alike, taking the esoteric seriously and in a balanced and responsible manner.

And in his peroration to the weekend:

> For me, there is no field of human concern or activity in which the Light of Christ does not shine. The deeper I go and the further I look, the more brightly does the light shine. I have come to be disquieted at the extent to which the Church in the West has become exotericised, externalised, over-rationalised and institutionalised until God himself is almost an academic concept, subject to the degrees, whims and fancies of learned dons! I am concerned that a field of human experience should have been pushed into the shadow, and all but consigned to him whom our Lord came to cast out! I am concerned too at the failure in communication between theology and the esoteric, and I am concerned that the theological and philosophical framework of occultism should so restrict the understanding of the occultist as to the uniqueness and true wonder of the Incarnation.
>
> The Qabalah, Jewish and Gentile, has much to say to us, and for me it has served as an invaluable frame of reference for my understanding of man and of the rest of creation; and it has brought me into a deeper wonder and adoration of Kether[5] himself, the source and author of all things, Jesus Christ, my Lord and my God.

This marked the end of the initial phase of our working together, that had started at Tewkesbury and continued through Parkend and Highnam, although I was to visit him from time to time at his various parishes in future years.

And so he departed for pastures new and a very different environment, not without a poetic glance back to Highnam, where he had learned and experienced so much. And with a certain prevision, did he but know it, of its future glory.

---

5   Kether = the Crown. Highest spiritual point on the Qabalistic Tree of Life.

Squire's Pew

Squire's Pew is where they keep the cleaning things;
the brooms and buckets, dustpan and its brush,
the flower-arranging crocks, the wire, the strings;
odd gloves, and things forgotten in the rush

to throw confetti at the latest bride.
Squire's pew is where they stacked the old hymn-books,
where ancient *tonic-sol-fa* Psalters hide,
and mouldy hassocks, fallen from their hooks.

Squire built this church to serve his own estates;
now Squire and tenants are all gone away.
The building, with its faithful handful, waits
another dawning, and another day.

5

NEWCASTLE

On 15th May 1973 I duly received a letter from St. John's Vicarage, Newcastle upon Tyne, to say they had arrived, that the move was as reasonable as these things ever were, save for one major nonsense, that the van was not big enough! Hence twenty tea chests, etc., etc., were still awaited.

Tony's Induction and Institution was scheduled for the morrow, and he was much looking forward to it and to being part of this congregation. Not that the Church had an obvious function at the moment. There could hardly have been a greater difference from a rural country parish, but he thought there was a great deal that it could and should be doing, one of them being bridge-building between orthodoxy and the fringes.

In a sense this had already begun as two "Jesus freaks" from Germany had turned up in the middle of the rehearsal and he found himself compelled to take them home for the night, much to the astonishment of the Church Wardens. That the Lord had sent them as a "try on" he had no doubt.

Whether the meths drinkers sleeping and urinating in the back pews of his inner city church came into quite the same bracket, I was not too sure. However, this was his take on it all:

St John's Church
Newcastle upon Tyne

When lightning strikes, it strikes the City here;
stone walls are strewn with human wrack,
door jambs are splintered, windows cracked,
yet glorious within. High all around
great temples to the gods of greed
soar skywards, bulge obscene.

No parish now. All out of place,
smoke-blackened, pilfered, old;
a shrine to fantasy perhaps, to fads
ecclesiastic? Yet for all that brings
a place to kneel before the Real:
the one still Centre at the heart of things.

Nonetheless, he found the North East as attractive as ever, as he had spent some of his boyhood there. He reported that St John's was quite a place! "<u>Five</u> power points: one under the nave altar, one under the curate's stall in the chancel, one under a pew in the nave, one in the corner of the North Transept and another under the wall in the corner of the South Transept. A perfect cross!"

The church had been consecrated in 1145-1245, and boasted a 15th century font cover, a Jacobean pulpit and 18th century altar slab, whilst the Lady Chapel contained a window including fragments of glass with the earliest known representation of the arms of Newcastle.

I was able to report back that things in my life seemed to divide between pre-Hawkwood and post-Hawkwood, an event that had certainly marked a watershed as far as I was concerned. I had decided to abandon any thought of introducing new teaching to the Helios course and on the Sunday afternoon of that weekend had met a promising couple who were able and willing to help me set up a completely new course organisation. All I had to do was write a text book for it!

He replied that he was not a bit surprised that life was "post" or "pre" Hawkwood. According to his perception he felt "the whole house shook!" Anyhow, his own *Priesthood of Man* should be out before long, and might well cause an upset in rather different circles.

In the meantime he found Newcastle the right place to be, the people very friendly and very, very active. The main drawback so far was lack of sleep, so he was praying for a "second wind." Work had been fast and furious but the real burden – almost the only real problem other than routine ones – was the hellish overdraft that had followed them from Highnam. But as all the other burdens from there had dropped away no doubt in time this one would too. There must be a pattern, he thought, a "curious dynamic" at work, but rather wished it would work faster! Highnam had, he supposed, to be hell for them in some respects because so much of the heavenly happened there too in another dimension.

Newcastle was a more "normal" place and felt like a five-year job to him, though in this bracing North East climate, the thought of *Sword in the Sun* frightened him to death. It might be publishable one day, but not yet. It might act as a quarry for material suitable for a specific public and indeed he gave me permission to quote extracts from it for *Experience of the Inner Worlds*, the book for my own course on the Christian Qabalah that I was currently writing. At the same time he was preparing lectures for another conference on Iona – "all about the Charismatic Movement etc., etc. Who knows what might happen? That could be a kind of Pentecostal hot seat – the mind boggles!".

In the meantime, *The Aryan Path,* a journal of the Theosophical Society in India, had come up with a most favourable review of *The Lord of the Dance,* calling it "an awesome exploration of mystical landscapes in the very depths of the soul and at the very heart of the Christian understanding of God, Man, and the cosmos."

> Mysticism has never been a central feature of the English religious tradition. This distinctive form of spiritual experience, though universal in its incidence among the world's major religions, is not evenly spread geographically or culturally, and in this respect England has been the poorer, compared with its Continental neighbours. If Julian of Norwich and Richard Rolle give evidence that medieval England was not without

its exponents of the mystical way, it was a small school when set alongside Master Eckhart and the Rhineland Mystics; the phenonomen was not absent from England's Reformation, but there was no Jacob Boehme.

This lack was continued: except for the margins of Anglo-Catholicism, English mainstream Christianity has had little room for mysticism, and has been the poorer for it. The Rev. Anthony Duncan, an Anglican priest, is therefore quite distinctive. His "inspirational" writings are not in the mode of conventional Christian piety or popular devotion, but rather are awesome explorations of mystical landscapes in the very depths of the soul and at the very heart of the Christian understanding of God, Man, and the cosmos. *The Lord of the Dance*, Duncan's latest essay in mysticism, defies easy review. In summary, it penetrates five major themes of the God-man relationship: 'The Great Dance,' 'Light,' 'Contemplation,' 'The Silence of Heaven' and 'I AM the Mind of All.'

The first sees man in his relationship to the Creator, and himself as part of the greater creation, visible and invisible, earthly and heavenly: "The Dance itself is the expression of the Mind of the Creator, it represents the whole pattern of Divine thought."

'Light' is a moving essay in the true tradition of light-mysticism: "Divinity is of the nature of Light; and where light shines, there may man see God, for the Divine nature is in the light itself by which he sees."

Evil in the world results from demonic forces, 'the Fallen Angel,' seen by the author as "a consciousness in great, subjective torment." In his study of 'Contemplation,' he describes the use of creative symbols and sensitive, spiritually aware imagination to lead the soul into higher and fuller planes of existence, towards the fulfilment of its spiritual vocation. In 'The Silence of Heaven' the mystery of the Eucharist is seen as the centre of God's cosmic activity, and 'activity which transcends many different planes of being': in this, man and the heavenly hierarchies are united with God.

The final essay, 'I AM the Mind of All,' is remarkable for the simplicity and power of its insights. This is a book containing much that is sublime, one to be pondered, reflected upon, and prayed with. Mr. Anthony Duncan is also the author of a well-known work in *The Christ, Psychotherapy & Magic*.

For all that *The Christ, Psychotherapy & Magic* had been somewhat critical of Theosophical influence on modern occultism it was something of an irony to find such a well informed and sympathetic appreciation of *The Lord of the Dance* from a Theosophical journal.

Which all goes to show that one cannot, in this game, make facile judgements based upon people's organisational affiliations.

Meanwhile, something of a reaction could well be expected in ecclesiastic circles about *The Priesthood of Man* which Bles were about to publish. Although I had read through the manuscript in the course of its writing I had not quite realised how revolutionary parts of it would seem, but the conservative style of its presentation made it something of a wolf in sheep's clothing.

The chapters likely to shock, frighten or offend the orthodox were, however, pointed out in the preface, Chapters 13, 23 and 24. They might cause some eyebrows to rise, the author said, but he was committed to what he had written.

In fact they contained much the same material as could be found in *The Sword in the Sun*. Chapter 13, entitled *The Way Things Are*, was a vast cosmic sweep based upon the spiritual evolutionary ideas of Teilhard de Chardin, and concerned the Fall of Man, one consequence of which was to narrow down mankind's awareness of the cosmos to the material plane only, in ignorance of the inner planes of creation.

> Plato gave expression to a similar concept and called it Atlantis. ...Like Eden, like the land referred to as the "Dream Time", Atlantis certainly existed as an historical fact, but on another wavelength. All these concepts are different subjective clothings for the same folk memory of the real world, of the unfallen wavelength, from which man is now exiled and to which, in the old way, he can never now return.

The "new way" of return, or universal redemption, Tony Duncan proclaimed was the earthly Incarnation of Jesus Christ, the great Redeemer.

This might well have passed as somewhat abstract speculation, but in Chapter 23 *A Chapter of Unfamiliar Affirmations* and Chapter 24 *Within the Within, or Beyond?* he nailed his colours to the mast.

The first took the issue of reincarnation head on.

> Reincarnation (or Rebirth) is an integral part of the nature of the created order as man knows it. It is part of the process of evolution, and it is the means whereby souls evolve in the natural order. This is the case not only with men, but also with all living creatures at every level of evolution. It is the way of creaturely perfection in the natural order.
>
> The evolution of man, as a spiritual being – his way of perfection in

the Natural order – has been by constant rebirth since his arrival on this wavelength. Thus, in general terms, the instinctual beliefs of Hinduism, Buddhism and some other religious systems are correct. This instinctual belief was not given to the Jews of the Old Testament. Their vocation was to receive the awareness of the historical process, and for this reason Our Lord had no occasion to make specific reference to this. (Such a reference would, in fact, have clouded the issues with which he dealt.) It is only now that it is necessary for Christians to come to terms with the reality of rebirth, and discover its implications in respect of the Christian Revelation.

Christ came, as he said, "not to destroy but to fulfil". He spoke not only of the Jewish Law, but of every Law of Nature, and included in them is the law of rebirth. For a believer, baptised into Christ, the necessity of rebirth is done away. He is perfected, not by Nature, but by Grace. Grace perfects and transcends Nature; there is no further need for rebirth. Evolution is fulfilled in the Baptised.

As a high church Anglican, Tony Duncan based his faith on the power of the Holy Sacraments, particularly that of Baptism, even if bestowed in infancy. But it was still possible to fall back from it.

> …The Baptised have no further need for rebirth, for Baptism is objective, it confers an altogether other order of being upon man. But man can fall from the Life of Grace, into which he has been baptised, back to the life of Nature. This he can do by deliberate choice – his own choice – either by unrepented Mortal Sin, or by virtue of the whole tenor of the life he chooses to lead. He may, of his own free will, become as if he had never been Baptised. During his current life on earth, he may repent of either case, and be freely restored to Grace. After his death to this life, however, the opportunity of repentance has passed and he must return to the life of Nature, to be subsequently reborn, bearing with him the consequences of his choice according to that principle generally known to men as Karma. In subsequent lives, he will get other opportunities for Baptism which he will accept or not according to the free will God gave him.

And he had worked out possible exceptions to this rule, to account for those who voluntarily returned even though without personal need to.

> Although the Baptised have no further need to return to this wavelength, many do in fact return, voluntarily and of their own free will. Indeed some may return many times. They do so for two reasons:

> The first is in order to realise for themselves the fullness won for them by Christ. This is the reincarnation of devotion to Almighty God. It is a free act of love, never an act of reparation. It is impossible for man to make reparation to God.
>
> The second is in order to perform a specific ministry to the Glory of God and the salvation of souls. In either case, the Baptised make themselves vulnerable to all the influences of the incarnate human wavelength. They do not always reincarnate in a Christian society and they may not, consciously, be Christians during this new life. But their Baptism transcends all subsequent incarnations because they are in Christ. They may, however, fall from Grace in this new life, and, reverting to Nature, become as if they had never been baptised. Some do so revert. Not many, but some. The danger is ever present. They are greatly helped by their discarnate brethren, but their free will is inviolate, and they can choose Nature rather than Grace.

This position presupposed the pre-existence of human souls, and that the spirit is neither masculine nor feminine, but androgyne, which is what Jesus meant when he said that there is neither marriage nor giving marriage in heaven, but that all are as the angels.

And in his penultimate chapter *Within the Within, or Beyond?* he took up the issue of communication between the planes, citing evidence for them in the bestowal of the Gifts of the Holy Spirit in the early church as described by St Paul in his first letter to the Corinthians (*chapter 12, verses 7 – 11*). He observed that it was astonishing how this passage could be read over and over again through the years, without its full import being realised. But that in modern terms, among the gifts listed, could be recognised mediumship of many kinds, charismatic healing and various other "psychic phenomena". None of which were looked upon with favour by ecclesiastical orthodoxy in the Western Church today. These gifts are objective and real, and are not limited to the Baptised.

> ...The Western Church has always inclined towards an over-paternalistic, over-institutionalised and over-legalistic endeavour to protect people from themselves and to inhibit the exercise of anything which might involve danger to faith and order and damage to souls. This is temperamental, but it is also unfaithful. Officially, the exercise of the perceptive gifts has been recognised only in tightly controlled situations. Within this climate, both St John of the Cross and St Teresa, highly endowed though they were, preferred to 'play down' the perceptive gifts.

> ...The fact is that communication from other planes of being – from souls, that is, who are no longer in this life – is a reality, and a reality beyond reasonable doubt to those who have studied the evidence. At best, it is a part of the Risen Life which can be described as "the practice of the Communion of Saints".

It was, he insisted, for persons in this life, something that was most typically given rather than sought, and a practice that at its best needed to be applied with considerable caution. For at less than its best it could justly be described in terms very different indeed. Integrity, right intention, the responsible and prayerful use of the gift and the context in which it was used were of overriding importance.

It was indeed fully as desirable with this as it was desirable, when using a radio set, to know where the programme is coming from! An analogy which he spelled out elsewhere in another poem.

WAVES AND VIBRATIONS

I am shot through by waves, vibrations;
and my world is pierced and penetrate
by worlds alternative, realities unseen
beyond my inner teaching. I may rise
upon their planes by apparatus, and a touch
will manifest their wonders on a screen.

I am shot through by wavelengths other,
half-glimpsed upon harmonics and half-known.
The apparatus is within, half-trusted, feared
lest it deceive, open what doors to what and whom?
To try the lock! To spring! To dree what weird;
erupt what nymphs and satyres in my drawing-room?

Anyhow, he concluded, there were those around who were appropriately attuned to such waves and vibrations, and responsibly so.

> ...There are very many gifted and dedicated persons who practice it with great devotion and with impressive sincerity. There is much, in occult science, which is of considerable worth and many important truths are enshrined therein ... a very great deal of occult tradition is both true and manifestly so. The Qabalah, the philosophical "map" of the general

structure of the Within of creation – and I fancy more so in its Gentile, occult form than in its far more devotional Jewish original. But magic, the art of making changes in consciousness in accordance with the will, is a "lower pyramid" exercise only. Its fulfilment is in Christ – but then it is no longer magic!

As might be expected, the *Church Times* raised its critical eyebrows considerably at much of this. "*A decidedly odd book, many readers may well think, to come from the pen of a priest of ten years' standing,*" sniffed its reviewer, but after a reasonably full précis of its contents conceded:

> That there is an element of the genuinely mystical, springing from personal experience, in these pages it would be churlish and stupid to deny. Some people may find them helpful, exciting and spiritually edifying. Others must be prepared for bewilderment. What is beyond contradiction is that this priest of the Church has written a book which, on any reckoning, is very unusual indeed.

Which I suppose, just about sums it up.

It is possible to see the strong influence of Iona upon much that he had written, material which was pretty well accepted in responsible spiritual circles that ventured a little beyond accepted orthodoxy, such as the Wrekin Trust or Hawkwood College, to say nothing of the dialogue between Tony Duncan and me over the past seven or eight years. He was much encouraged by its reception in the wider world beyond ecclesia:

> I got a splendid review in *Books and Bookmen* the other day. At last someone <u>likes</u> *Priesthood of Man* – not an ecclesiastic! He kept calling me "intelligent" for two pages. Obviously a clever chap himself! There is a tremendous lot bubbling up at the moment and I find the times vastly exciting. Even the institutional Church is (under pressure of inflation from the Lord) thinking about possibilities of all kinds that would not have been given a thought eighteen months ago.

There was naturally a more mundane side, and a considerable one, to Tony Duncan's role as vicar of an inner city church, some of which is reflected in his poems. The vicarage was in quite a rough old area, in Summerhill Grove, not far from an old convent, from which the nuns were fast departing.

WEST END

Turn right at night upon the doorstep leaving;
the littered lamppost lighting, all shall then be well
out to the steep hill, down long dereliction down
past motor bikes and sex, dog-guarded stolen things;
the sleazy shop fronts sliding to the heart of town.

Turn left at your own peril, up towards the thieving;
the shaven-headed gangs of girls, by hell
instructed, kicking, slashing. Echoing their shriek
the dingy walls. In shadows, past the fitful rings
of light, two muggers linger, waiting for the weak.

And now the convent's closing, nuns are leaving.
Convent and vicarage; the vagrants ring one bell
and then the other, five doors down the street.
The square, long raddled, still to grandeur clings;
now menaced by a dark despair it was not made to meet.

And not all was confined to the delinquent young, to the derelict or to petty criminals. There were more well heeled and vicious elements around.

THE GROVE

He hurled the petrol up the wooden stair,
leaned round the door, threw in a match.
The cobbles bounced his footfalls from the walls.
a car door slammed, an engine roared.
The tall old terrace house was in his name;
he settled down to draft it: the insurance claim.

I woke to diesel engines, flashing lights, the glare;
looked out to ladders looming up to snatch
six old and broken men, and heard their calls
from single rooms, rack-rented, without board.
They paid his claim. He revelled in the fun;
repaired the first house, bought another one.

Nonetheless he maintained a philosophic, not to say theological, overview of it all in his vision of the different levels of this, or any other town, each potentially a holy city as William Blake might well have seen.

Three Towns

The town beneath the town lives on,
a shadow life. Infections as from drains
stopped up make subtle sicknesses,
some fatal. Others cloud the looking
or make hearing hard. The town above
the town beneath lives now, but dangerously.

A town about the town lives through;
Earth-bound, a muted heaven, seeks
to rise, can rise so high, no more;
still rooted in the town's own time
but on another scale. The town wove through
the town about lives now, precariously.

A City these three towns transcends
and runs them through with unseen flash
of Uncreated Light. Thus threaded
on Love's needle, side by side,
three towns in one unknowingly abide
'till Light transfigure them, eternally.

Nonetheless all was something of a contrast from country parishes in the past.

> On Monday morning I found a terrified, hungry 70% Whippet puppy tied to a bench outside the vestry door. One thing led to another, and now we have Ferdinand, Benedict, Emma – and Flopsy! Cats as before.

Which is perhaps an opportunity to record that a canine population, usually King Charles spaniels, was ever a part of the Duncan household, and from whom, as with Balaam's dog, lessons in life could be drawn.

Dog

The lightest touch of knife upon a plate,
faint rustling of paper, sound of tin
or lid manipulated from within
the furthest room or, strangest to relate,
remotest contemplation of a state
which manifests these things; wherein –
from silence fit for dropping of a pin,
deep sleep to wide awake – Dog supplicates!

The furry face accuses, gazes, pleads,
blackmails, implores, glances from face to face
(lest tit-bits chance to change their destination)
to represent Priority, and Needs.
Such single-minded running of the race
puts Man to shame for simple application.

Tony, Helga and friends

Meanwhile, Mowbrays, a prestigious and well established religious publishing house, had approached Tony Duncan looking for a book on occultism! This he duly signed up to under the title of *The Fourth Dimension*. It was the first book he had actually been commissioned to do, and to his pleasant surprise it sold well when it appeared at the end of 1975. It attracted a very favourable postbag too (on the whole!) along with three appearances on local radio. A fair number of his acquaintances, including some Roman Catholic priests, had purchased a copy, and he felt that he had somehow plugged a gap.

Subtitled *A Christian approach to the occult* on the cover and *A Christian view of occultism* on the title page, this 125 page paperback was, in my view, a masterly attempt at explaining occultism to the general public. As he explained in the preface:

> Occultism is a dark subject to the majority of Christians, both clerical and lay, and "the occult" has become a dirty word among us. And yet, quite suddenly, it is becoming a respectable option in society; the bookshops are full of paperbacks on witchcraft, astrology and "do-it-yourself" occultism of all kinds, witches appear on television, the names of well-known mediums become almost household words, and the Church's reaction is seen, all too often, to be in negative terms.
>
> Indeed it sometimes appears that the Church is obliged to react rather than to take action in the first instance. And too many of us do not know what we are talking about when we do pronounce upon the subject. What is occultism? How big a subject is it? What makes its devotees tick? What kind of people are they, and has the subject a serious side to it as well as a sensationalist one? These are the questions which this book will seek to answer.

And answer them he did. He distinguished three main groups of people within the occult world.

The first containing people from all walks of life who happen to be psychically sensitive, naturally clairvoyant or perceptive in some other way. Indeed apart from himself, he had one or two friends who came into this category. One, whom he cited, who had a gift for curing minor ailments by a laying on of hands.

The second group those specifically interested in the serious practice of magic as a science and an art, most of whom would regard themselves as "white" magicians as opposed to the perversion and misuse of these practices, generally labelled as black magic.

And thirdly a great multitude of "dabblers in the occult" who constitute a far greater hazard both to themselves and to other persons than they realise, and from among whose ranks most of the casualties from occult practice were to be found.

He pointed out that much of this was a reaction from barren 18th century rationalism, beginning with the romantic movement that had developed on many fronts, bringing about a revival of the great mystical tradition of the Church on the one hand, along with a resurgence of what was known to its students as the Western Mystery Tradition. Taking up the middle ground had been a remarkable flowering of a type of "adult fantasy" fiction of which George Macdonald, C.S.Lewis and J.R.R.Tolkien were perhaps the authors most widely known. Whilst an encounter with Oriental religious traditions had brought into being a number of Theosophical groups. It was simply not possible to pass grand, sweeping judgements upon this vast field.

Most importantly, the twentieth century had seen the emergence of three great men whose work made possible the establishment of communication between occultist and theologian. These three being the Jesuit palaeontologist Pierre Teilhard de Chardin, the psychologist Carl Gustav Jung and the "spiritual scientist" Rudolf Steiner.

However, to the majority of people, clerical and lay, the Occult was not the ordered, philosophically based intuitivism of the more responsible practitioners. It was seen through the more prominent, vain, sensation-seeking approach of dabblers in the subject, who were as much a matter of irritation and disgust to the dedicated esotericist as they were to the clergy who were often called to clear up the mess they could leave. Of the three groups he had earlier defined this group was the largest of all.

Yet there was much that was positive and healthy, and with obvious potential in what might be described as the "meditation movement" which was attracting large numbers of young people.

In this respect I recall a comment he made some years before, after visiting an event in Glastonbury along with the Diocesan Youth Chaplain, who, after seeing 2000 youngsters a day being taught meditation by a Hindu "holy man", turned and said to him "It's about time we pulled our fingers out and got on with our *proper* job, isn't it?"

More immediately, after some agonising on both our parts, I had got round to signing him up to publish *The Sword in the Sun* using the pen name of Douglas Warren. His agreement to a pen name was something of a shift in perspective from Highnam days, but he was beginning to go through something of a spiritual crisis and a reassessment as to what he could or should be doing in his pastoral, writing and mystical life. He had even become rather doubtful about publishing *The Sword in the Sun* at all. He had a soft spot for it because it was so intensely personal, but doubted if it would do much beyond making him a cult-object for "a few blue rinses" and encourage a credibility gap just where one ought not to be – in the still rationalist dominated Western Church. Although its time would come, he was sure.

As it was, the decision was taken out of our hands as a massive bill from the Inland Revenue for unpaid corporation tax caught up with me and clipped my publishing wings for a bit, and in the end it was almost another twenty years before *The Sword in the Sun* appeared, and then in the United States of America.

Nonetheless he was much encouraged when I told him about my being invited to talk to a student society at Cambridge University where the organisers said they had been greatly enthused by *The Lord of the Dance* and were thinking of asking him down too.

I had in the meantime completed my student textbook *Experience of the Inner Worlds* and sent him a copy of the manuscript. He was immensely pleased with it, and thought it first class and "terrific stuff".

> Couldn't put it down! Full marks! I should love to see this reviewed in due time by a competent reviewer (if one could be found) in a sensible theological journal. (They might twitch a bit at Chapter 10!) But this is quite splendid and ought to go a long way towards restoring the balance of things on the occult front.

He was, not unnaturally, moved by the fact that it was structured upon, and featured quotations from, *The Lord of the Dance* and *The Sword in the Sun* and concluded with some words if his angel:

> A man would search for God?
> Let him beware!
> He will discover his true self.
> A man would seek himself?
> Let him beware!
> He is in mortal peril of beholding God!

A main feature of the book was its coverage of the history of various aspects of occultism and mysticism over the centuries. This came about because although I regarded the monthly exercises – inspired by *The Lord of the Dance* – to be the most important part of the book, I needed a chapter of text to accompany each one and occupy the student's mind with something reasonably relevant. It fell out quite naturally that this could best be done on an historical basis.

This, after its publication in 1975, led to further opportunities. The publishing director of Mowbrays, having been encouraged with the reception of *The Fourth Dimension,* asked Tony Duncan if he would try writing "a fairly definitive history of white magic". Or if he felt this beyond him, to recommend someone who could. As I had clearly done a lot of research in this direction, Tony, backed up by Dom Robert Petitpierre, replied that I would be the natural choice. Consequently the job came my way, and *A History of White Magic* duly appeared in 1978 (later published in the United States as *Magic and the Western Mind*).

But 1977 had been a difficult year for Tony Duncan. He had "a kind of mini-heart attack" just before Easter, which the doctor put down to stress and overwork, and in the Autumn became "quite agitated", as he described it, about "having a go" at a university degree. The high intellectual flying of some of his congregation might well have sparked this impulse towards academe, and encouraged by a poetic "Chinese PhD who lectured in linguistics and was married to an Irish PhD who lectured in Sanskrit," he had also begun to write poetry again.

He had since had "some eloquent and almost tearful" rejection slips from a couple of Scottish publishers following attempts to get a collection accepted, but the Cowley Fathers had done him proud, with three poems in five issues of their journal *New Fire* which he thought not bad going. One of which was the following.

Healer and Patient

An angel stands before a blindfold man
who cries: "There are no angels in Creation!
I have disproved them all with my philosophy
and made of them a turn of speech,
outmoded in our day and age. Necessity
no doubt for man before my critical approach,
subjecting all things to the sharpest minds
and clearest sight of reason and theology,
had liberated mankind from a dead mythology."

"What will he do?" the angel asked,
"when I take off the blindfold and he sees!"
The Lord replied; "Be gentle! He has basked
in human cleverness these many years
and thinks he does it for my sake! Be gentle.
The Light will dazzle him. Respect his tears."

He was accepted as an external student for a Bachelor of Divinity degree by London University, attended some interesting lectures from some of his congregation at Newcastle University, and enrolled at Wolsey Hall correspondence college to learn Greek.

Or, as he put it,

> I am learning Greek. To be truthful I am wallowing in Hellenic hieroglyphs and wondering what the hell was the matter with these fools! (Why can't these beastly abroad people speak English like everybody else etc. etc. etc.) The rest of it is almost plain sailing, with the odd rock here and there, but Greek…I shall have to be at the poetry again.
>
> The degree mania is, I think, the beginning of a new something-or-other. At the least, it is a going back to school which will stop me beginning to mentally free-wheel towards retirement – or some such nonsense as that. … (But as I don't qualify for a full pension until I am 72…!) There are more books to be written, I think. And better ones. Who knows, there might even be more bridges to build, with all the posthumous appreciation that goes with that field of endeavour!

He finished off by translating the nursery rhyme "Mary had a little lamb" into Greek. *"Jolly impressive,"* he remarked, *"if you don't know Greek!"* And as I did not, I was indeed duly impressed!

Despite his up-beat tone it later appeared that his last year at Newcastle became something of an increasing strain, including the death of Big Black Cat and two of the dogs, Ferdinand of old age, and Flopsy in a road accident, and also with the children leaving home for institutions of higher learning.

It may have been at this time that he wrote some of his darker poems revealing some of the stresses upon a minister of the church treading a fine line between his mystical and psychical awareness and the more conventional expectations made of him. But there ever shone through them a bright faith in heavenly realities.

This might be in his role as priest:

The Priest in Retrospect

Oh! I am vulnerable enough, God knows!
I have no need for itching shoulder-blades
in whom a trusted comrade's blade still shows
scar-tissue, livid, here and there. Betrayed,
but what of that? Blood-stained, the water flows
under some bridge now long forgot. Re-made
by murder! The assassin's in my heart;
more vulnerable yet to Cupid's dart!

I am respectable enough, God knows,
to flutter the lace curtains as I pass
should madness overtake me, and expose
a mind all de-conditioned, clear as glass
unstained, where arched and figured, tinted rose
and faculty-approved, once shrined the Mass.
But Mass and Mystery, transcending quite,
prepare these eyes for Uncreated Light.

Oh! I am vulnerable enough, God knows,
to write down boldly what I've seen, have seen,
and have been told because I'm old, God knows,
and profit nothing more by what I've been.
And profit nothing shall in these last throws
of Heaven's dice before it all comes clean
and *is*, and *is*, and *is* eternally.
When you and I, and everything, shall *be*.

The Mass Priest

No, I am not a pulpit preaching man,
all high and lifted up and fenced about;
stockaded by stout timbers or by stone,
my head above the parapet alone,
all beetle-browed, the pious pews to scan,
convict of sin, of certainties to shout.

If I must speak, then I must stand alone
and vulnerable, and look them in the eye
whom I presume to lecture, or suggest
such things as shall pertain to their heart's rest.
For Christ was vulnerable and stood alone,
an easy aim; was quite prepared to die.

Or as prophet:

THE PROPHET IN FRUSTRATION

Oh! I have done with barren argument,
with seeking to convince the tight-shut mind,
the tunnel-vision that will not relent
or open wide lest it some monster find,
advancing to devour with fixed intent,
all hell-instructed. They feel safer, blind,
and look askance, cannot relate to me,
who cannot bear to look, lest they should see.

Religion! With your law which fuels our fears
and rules all reason with your iron rod –
relax! For look! The swirling darkness clears
would we but just abide. No! Iron-shod,
intransigent! The vision disappears.
Religion sits upon the throne of God
where hierarchs and their flocks would have it be,
who cannot bear to look, lest they should see.

The All-Transcending has transcended quite;
irradiates all thoughts within His Mind.
Transfiguration is to left and right
and all about us all, who stand here, blind.
The End is come, Beginning is in sight;
beginningless and endlessness behind!
All Heaven shouts at us to wake, and *be*,
who cannot bear to look, lest we should see.

Or as mystic:

The Mystic Mystified

With Heaven's cap and bells upon my head
all falls into absurdity. My place:
a blindfold man who knows not where to tread,
is steered by unseen hands, with time and space
so spun in timelessness I lose the thread.
For all that was, and is, now gathers pace;
a three-ring circus, where the ages prance
and all's caught up in the Eternal Dance.

Kaleidoscope am I, where all collides
within my consciousness, and falls to bits.
What can I do but laugh? For truth resides
in fallen men who fall about in fits
and know themselves absurd. The mind – it sits
at ease with metaphor. The changing tides
then sweep the pieces into patterns new;
the rhythms change to dance me in on cue.

I know not who I am, what shall ensue,
who have identity and place assured
but live by glimpses, fragments of a view;
who, wearing motley, have to Heaven soared;
now cragfast, given little things to do
pertaining – as I hope – unto the Lord.
The very Universe summed-up and gone,
I do the shopping, put the kettle on.

Or in the hurly burly of parish duties:

On the Press of Irrelevance

The things that matter are so very few
and fewer by the year; and yet remain
so many, many busy things to do
to satisfy the senses, dull the pain

of the irrelevance of much of life,
the questionable purpose of our toil.
So little meaning in our daily strife,
while things peripheral contrive to spoil

health, happiness, our leisure and our peace.
And on we go, as year succeeds each year
ordering disorder that it cease;
that hierarchies of mattering appear.

The things that matter! But the other won't
comply; we're bondsmen to the things that don't!

And conscious of the double life between the interior and the exterior man:

Spiritual Warfare

I live my double life, who knows?
I humour all the hum-drum day,
my functions plain, fulfilled in part
or by intention. Darkness falls,
my battlefield. I sweat and suffer sore
while groping ever for the dawn to rest,
to rise once more. Time passes by;
the dark invades the daylight, welling up
to sudden nightmare. Down I must
into a fell destruction. Victory is won
but I must die that it be manifest
and go on daylight living, set apart,
misunderstood, unrecognized, at second best;
yet be not bitter, though it break my heart!

Or living up to others' expectations:

Growing Pains

Am I a threat to others if I change?
Is my *persona* but a guarantee,
gilt-edged security, that all shall be
and shall remain as ever was
nor nothing new be thought or spoke?

Is timelessness in midst of time
refrigerate? Is childhood
everlasting? I serve that others grow,
and I must learn to trust, I cannot know,
but minister, it seems, in chains. I choke!

Or ultimately, a veritable *cri de coeur* from the vulnerable and overworked individual:

The Priest

I am jealous of my space
and re-create it;
build up again my crumbled walls
and mend my inner fences;
take up the Quest of Timelessness,
that hidden recess of the heart
where God the Holy Spirit dwells;
regain my poise, my equilibrium
to take the next onrush of Time
and stay still standing on two feet
with mind in heart.

I need my space;
my life is other people
wanting things.

Some of these things being of doubtful relevance.

SILENCE IN HEAVEN

Diwali decorations fill
the shining Leicester shop fronts. Then,
as Hindu banknotes burst the till,
the same bright lights switch on again
for reindeer, and for Santa Claus,
for Seven Dwarfs and for Snow White,
a crib with angels shining bright,
all serving the commercial cause.

The shopping days to Christmas fly,
and Holy Church reflects the same.
Christingles and *Nine Lessons* vie
each to outplay the Christmas Game
from early Advent, putting on
for groups, and gatherings, and clubs,
and shops, and offices, and pubs,
roaring religious marathon.

The cause of all this noise and din?
The silence of one starlit sky
and, in the back-yard of an inn,
unutterably Mystery.
To grasp the point we lack the poise,
so folk-religion and the Church
embrace and stagger, trip and lurch
and celebrate it all with noise.

However, help was at hand and he and Helga were able to take some holidays in the high hills. Either in the Lake District:

The Lakeland Fells

I have climbed and walked upon the fells
as if all time itself was short
and these the foothills of eternity.

Unfailing rapture of the senses here
and of the heart. And here the space
to meet, to draw apart, to wonder and to be.

To walk the fells is to be changed.
I am forever changed; and no regrets
for self-consuming rapture sought;
for time itself was short.

Or in his beloved Scotland:

The Paps of Jura

Damp mist hangs heavily. A fitful rain
now comes, now goes. The hills are vanished deep
into their clouds and all the world's asleep.
The steaming cattle stand about the lane,
gaze into nowhere, watch the damp day wain;
while on the hillside, silently, the sheep
chew into timelessness; chew as if to keep
time timeless until light break through again.

Three hills lie hidden, lost in mist around,
soaring invisible; long lost, grey and cold
until the cloud shall lift and they be found.
Mysterious their beauty is, and old.
All unattainable: *Ben of the Sound,*
The Sacred Mountain, and *The Mount of Gold.* *

*(Beinn a'Chaolais, Beinn Shiantaidh, Beinn an Oir)

And gleaning lessons therefrom:

Root and Rock

Root and rock, crag-clinging tree,
tenuous and terrible, both fierce and frail
whose tender tendrils split the stone,
seek out and suck, adorn the precipice
with prettiness and grace; unspoiled you are,
for mankind's faulty functions, exemplar.

So perched and poised, precarious are we
in terror and in truculence; fated to fail
in fear and fantasy that we are all alone
to reign so royal in our own imagined edifice.
Good Nature! In our blunderings again, and yet again,
be patient. Be compassionate. And teach us to be men.

In his last letter to me from Newcastle in 1978 he wrote:

> We hope to go to Iona for three weeks at the beginning of August. After the holidays, with both boys already off our hands and Fifi in hopes of either Edinburgh or Liverpool Universities, and with the Harem [*a bevy of student lodgers*] dispersed, we shall be left with the animals and an uneasy feeling that it is time we moved on. But where? And to what? I am pretty sure that I have done my stint here and I don't feel that I have any more to give to this place – other than sheer routine if you understand me. And I am not a routine man.

And at the end of the year came the message:

> Surprise! Surprise! Surprise! After five and a half years in the City Centre we are moving to one of the most beautiful big villages/small towns in Northumberland, with a huge castle, a lovely Norman church, the river Coquet (famous for salmon) winding round the Georgian Vicarage, the sea half a mile away and the countryside beautiful. The move has come at the best possible time for all of us and we are very grateful but it will be a dreadful wrench actually leaving St. John's. But the family are all grown up and have started their own adult lives and so a move is a good new start for us.

6

WARKWORTH

Early in 1979 I received a joyful letter from Warkworth Vicarage, Morpeth, Northumberland to say that they had arrived between Christmas and the New Year in pouring rain, blizzard and ice. Tony felt as if he had been released from prison and was writing this (in haste, as usual) in front of a sea-coal and driftwood fire with the river Coquet rolling icily past the study window, and herons, "steeple-stemmed, spiring and spearing". (Dylan and Thomas and all that!)

He could not remember if he ever told me they were moving, but indeed could not remember much of the last six months. Briefly, the Bishop got the message that a break from the city centre would be a good idea and had offered him Warkworth with the words "you will be able to write the next two books!" He supposed he would now have to write two books to justify it. As it turned out, this was easier said than done, although he did manage to publish two books during his eight years at Warkworth, albeit one self published book of poems, *The Lover Within*, and the other compiling an anthology, *Jesus, Essential Readings*, for Aquarian Press.

Warkworth is an old Northumbrian village about a mile from the coast, almost completely surrounded by a loop in the River Coquet, and noted for its riverside walks, medieval castle and an ancient hermitage. In about 737 King Ceolwulf of Northumbria had given church and village to the abbot and monks of Lindisfarne, and the 12th century church of St Lawrence, built on the site of the old one, was of a size and dignity far beyond the needs of the present population. It had been the scene of a terrible massacre in 1174 when some 300 townsfolk seeking refuge from Scottish raiders were brutally put to the sword by Duncan, Earl of Fife.

Not too close a relation to his namesake we trust, although Tony Duncan was immensely proud of his Scottish ancestry, through his father, and could be quite poetically bellicose recalling the Jacobite rising and the battle of Culloden in 1746, in which his ancestors fought in the Atholl Brigade.

ATHOLL BRIGADE AT CULLODEN

It is some comfort that, alone of all
the rightful line you, right of line,
prevailed. When Keppoch fell and all was lost,
with Elcho's Life Guards and Fitzjames' Horse,
you, Campbell haunted on the flank,
stood fast and stopped proud Hawley in his ride,
held off the traitor and the Sassenach
long, almost long enough – and died.

You ventured all for putting back the clock,
and held it still for one brief, glorious day –
and lost. Then long and bitter was its chime.
I wondered as I stood beside your rock;
were you, now Prince and King have passed away,
perhaps two centuries before your time?

It is mentioned in an exchange he had with the angel in *The Sword in the Sun*.

ANGEL: You are a Scot, for all the English blood that is also in you. Tell me, what constitutes the essence of Scotland? Does it depend upon the people?

ME: No. It is the land itself. "I discern strange, silent, elemental things." The people conform to the land, it is that "elemental something" which has welded together Pict, Scot, Anglo-Saxon and Briton into an unmistakable whole. We are heirs to a "continuing something", but I wish I knew what it was.

The quotes he makes are from another poem of his which hints at these deeper things, along with the "clapping about me this after that, as if to wear about my body that which dwells, yet unrequited, in my heart" for he would, on occasion wear tartan kilt and highland regalia even back in Tewkesbury.

My Native Land

The Whore of Babylon it is
that keeps the two of us apart!
A monstrous idol of a thing
that slave-men call "Economy."
And so you must remain far off;
an image of that state from which
I am forever exile; a dream
of that with which I would identify,
and do identify, clapping about me
this after that, as if to wear
about my body that which dwells,
yet unrequited, in my heart.

What is this thing you are?
What is that essence which,
embracing and including all,
finds its expression in those dreams
that haunt and hurt my memory?
You are not human. I discern

WARKWORTH

strange, silent, elemental things;
perchance a king of Devic kings,
a multitude of little states
in which abide spirits of wood
and water, flower and field, and stone,
in deep and wonderful embrace.

I have heard their music on the mountain tops
and have had a grave and silent commerce
with the great, grey stones
who guard your secret kingdoms.
I have turned my careless feet away;
whispered a blessing and been blessed.

This undefined, this enigmatic thing;
this, your essential being, I would wed,
as those have wed who shine
about your holy places, and have wound
themselves and you about that golden thread
which holds his jewels on their maker's head;
His crown, and our eternity.

The medieval hermitage, about three quarters of a mile along the river from Warkworth castle, is accessible only by ferry boat. Carved out of the sandstone rock from what may originally have been a cave, and complete with rib vaulting, altar, sacristy and a couple of rooms believed to have been the hermit's living space. It first appears in the historical record in 1487 when a priest was appointed to say mass there, but there is an older tragic legend about the place – of Sir Bertram of Bothal, one of the knights of the Percy family who once lived in Warkworth castle before they removed to nearby Alnwick. Sir Bertram was betrothed to a lady Isobel but, in a bizarre story of mistaken identity, inadvertently killed her along with his own brother. After this it is said he gave all his goods to the poor and built the tiny hermitage in which he lived for the rest of his life.

Tony Duncan however sensed that the cave had a more remote and darker history, as a place of sacrifice to the river god. And its redemption to holy use inspired him to write some lines about it.

WARKWORTH HERMITAGE

A place of sacrifice to river gods,
of casting down. The smashed, the swallowed up
the river god devoured. All's changed;
a place of ancient lights which throw
their antique shadows on the crumbling walls,
all etched in damp in deepest darkness,
candle-sought. An ancient delving
into Mother Earth; a second womb
wherein to be reborn. All's changed;
the broken altar testifies: rebirth,
and Light transcending darkness. Late,
and later legend, a new cave
all churched and chapelled in the living rock,
fulfilling, yet obscuring, all the age-old stains.
The river god is quiet now. True sacrifice remains.

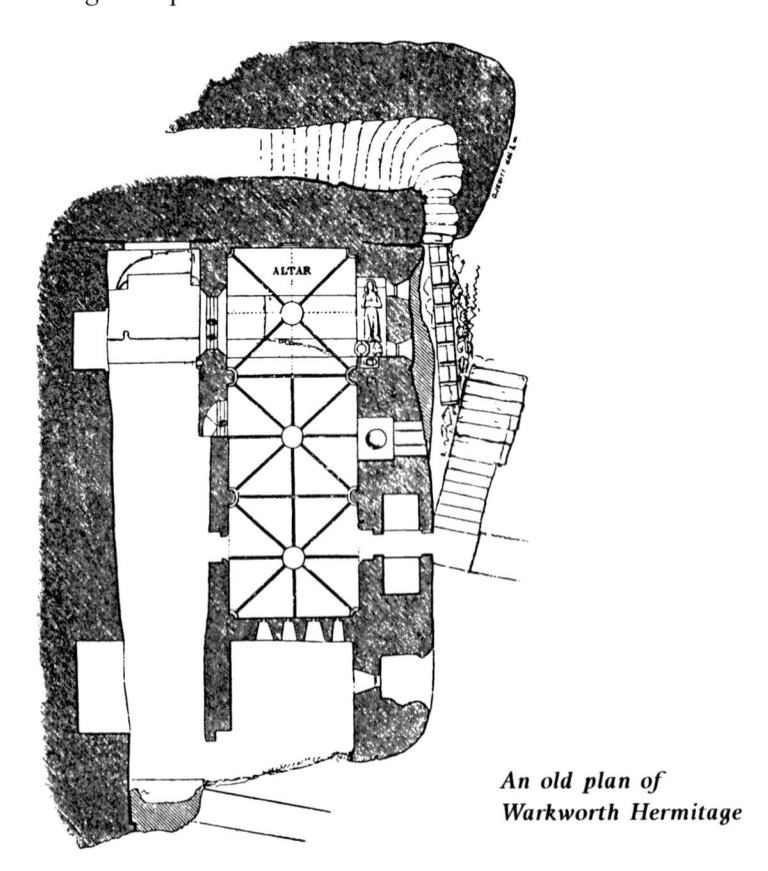

An old plan of Warkworth Hermitage

As was the practice with the Church of England, greatly overstretched with more parishes than priests at this time, he was allocated another parish, at Acklington, a small village grouped about a prison built on an old RAF airfield, a housing estate for the warders and their families, plus a few large farms and a second tiny village called Guyzance. But he found it a lively community and most enjoyable to be a part of. Like Warkworth it also had a church far out of proportion to its present needs, but which he revered nonetheless.

St John's Church, Acklington

The thing is quite absurd. Unviable
by all criteria of Church and World;
no place at all and nothing there.

Intangible, an unexpected Joy;
a place of peace and beauty, and of Love
a burning-glass. Where all is lost
and everything is found. Despair
of tidy little minds, town-bred.

Where Life wells up against the rules;
all wrong! Yet all that's right is dead!

So he was well pleased with his new location, found Warkworth to be beautiful, the house a gem, the church a Norman beauty, solid as a rock, and the community warm and friendly. The holy island of Lindisfarne nearby was worth a visit, although it had snowed or poured with rain each time they had been there save one, thus not good for picking up the "vibrations"! Although throughout the summer it vibrated with trippers, as, so they discovered, did Warkworth.

He was much taken with an advance copy of my *History of White Magic*, although felt it somewhat overpriced. Mowbrays had taken fright at the last minute about potential sales and upped the cover price in hopes of making something out of a highly discounted book club sale. Which, however, did not happen!

> It reads beautifully, is lucid and – to my way of thinking – conveys a balance which suggests not knowledge, nor even understanding, but wisdom. (You

seem to have hopped over the abyss!) I only hope that reviewers in the Church Press don't review it with the single word "Aaaaaaagh!" without reading it and thinking! And I would dearly love to see it descend from its £8.00 worth of hard covers to the paperback shelves of W.H.Smith.

I think two things stand out in my reading. The first is the Coleridge "imagination" thing which I feel is a vital insight. The second is the dolorous stroke, struck because of the positively demonic turn the religious power-structures had taken, which clove physical science away from its own soul and established the Universe as a Mechanism in men's minds instead of an Organism. If ever there was a second Fall from Grace it is here. And what a hotch-potch of psychism and eccentricity the whole scene has seemed to have become since then!

I think the book says some tremendously valuable things, and in a wholly admirable way. Whatever its commercial future (which I hope will be bright) it has uttered a word in the collective unconscious, and that is its first and most important task.

He was obviously still in there with his Qabalistic studies, as his reference to Knowledge, Understanding and Wisdom (in that order) alluded to the sequence of the higher spheres on the Tree of Life, Daath, Binah and Chokmah. The Coleridgean theory of the imagination was hardly my invention, as I had first gleaned it from Bernard Nesfield-Cookson, principal of Hawkood College and keen student of Rudolf Steiner, William Blake and Teilhard de Chardin.

As Kathleen Raine had pointed out in a foreword:

"Magic" is a word whose associations are both glamorous and sinister; Gareth Knight, well known to his readers as the most down-to-earth and pragmatic of magicians, by seeking to show what magic really is and to what body of thought it belongs, dissipates both these illusions. At the same time he shows how real is the world upon whose laws the operation of "magic" (and of prayer for that matter) depend. It is the world of "imagination", consciousness itself, the secret *prima materia* of the alchemists. Imagination (he uses the word in Coleridge's sense and Blake's) is none the less real because it cannot be quantified. It is a radical fallacy of materialism that there are in the world differences only of degree, but between the quantifiable world of matter and the world of consciousness there is a difference in kind; the one can never be described or understood in terms of the other. What Coleridge calls "facts of mind" constitute no part of quantifiable scientific knowledge, but they are none the less real…

> The soul has too long been crushed between the upper millstone of the Church's abstract discursive theology (based upon philosophy of Aristotle) and the nether millstone of scientific materialism. A renewed attention to the world of imagination (the soul's native and proper element) is an important aspect of what Yeats foresaw as "the rise of soul against intellect now beginning in the world."

Tony was still plodding away at a London University degree but beginning to find New Testament Greek by correspondence course no joke. Whilst the whole endeavour had seemed important while he was at Newcastle, "almost as a means to holding on to my own life", here in Warkworth that imperative slipped away. And was further provoked when SPCK began to bring out a 60 volume series of *Classics of Western Mysticism and Spirituality*. As soon as he saw the advertisement he got a jolt to the effect "Get it!" and was having the volumes sent to him as they came out – four at a time.

He found this very worthwhile and "more important than doing undergraduate essays on nit-picking points of criticism" that had kept him going during his last year at Newcastle. More important was the discovery of kindred spirits among the writers of the spiritual classics. That is to say – as *people*. What they wrote either turned him on or left him cold (although never *quite* cold).

He discovered a soft spot for the self tutored 17th century Qabalistically inspired Protestant visionary Jacob Boehme – who had been forbidden to publish his work because the local Lutheran pastor didn't like it. Also his English follower, the 18th century William Law, who was thought acceptable when he wrote the *Serious Call to a Devout and Holy Life* but rather fell from favour when he turned to *The Spirit of Love*. The rabbis too, Nahman of Brastlav and Abraham Isaac Kook rather appealed to him, and he was looking forward to some Qabalistic texts, including *The Zohar*, that were due to follow.

In his new found freedom as a country parson again he was keen to get on with some more writing, but was not quite sure of which way to go. However, he cast his net wide and was even having a go at a children's story.

> Oh yes! While dozing away an hour's journey in the front of a funeral car on its way to the crematorium, I half-wrote (in my mind) a book for grown-up children. It is all about a diminutive teddy-bear who has served as a nose-weight in several of my balsa-and-tissue-paper gliders, and who has, in consequence, something of a passion for aviation. I have about 1000 words furtively on paper already, they will be backed up by snapshots. He and a fellow bear (assisted by two stuffed mice) are busily building an aeroplane at this very moment. If you will pardon me, I must go and give them a hand!

His enthusiasm for model aircraft has already been hinted at in his verses about sloping off from Highnam with the doctor and the dentist to the Exhibition of Model Engineers. A couple of other poems reveal his youthful interest in aviation, including qualifying as a glider pilot.

THE AERODROME

A yellow windsock was my prayer-flag then;
and wood, and wire, and canvas, and the smell
of oil my sacraments; external signs
of inner flight, tools of my trade
and marks of calling. Leather helmets
and green grass; propellers, wood,
two-bladed, swung by hand, and bark
of engine catching; these my life,
my whole significance on summer days
set free from sea and shingle beach.
And stimulated. Not the world of me –
grey flannel bags, moustaches and clipped speech –
but flying; ever upwards like the lark
into an everlasting summer haze.

Warkworth

Ticket Hop

A jerk and a rumble. The mile-long line
taut, tugs and trembles at its panting pace;
then silence. The horizon falls, the field
aslant, slips by the tail and out of sight
and I am left in solitude, in ecstasy of flight.

No instrument but instinct once the line's let fall;
in motion motionless, a patchwork sliding past.
One flesh with canvas, plywood and the whispering wires,
an Icarus incarnate, soaring ever in the sun;
fulfilment of my schooldays, here my manhood is begun.

Now crosswind caught, the boundary closes fast;
instinct untaught, inspired of adoration
turns on a wingtip once, once more,
sinks soft to grass, on wingtip gently laid.
Congratulations! Wings! Alas! I never flew again.

Towards the end of 1979, having been at Warkworth for a year, he said it felt, in some ways, like only a few weeks, but in other ways as if they had been there all their lives. They loved living there, the village was beautiful, it was a very happy community and a remarkably lively one. The Vicarage garden was big enough and manageable, the river winding round two sides of it, and the outlook all round could not be more delightful. With the sea only 20 minutes walk from the vicarage door their dogs had never had it so good, with their five mile walks to the sea and along the sands, in and out of the dunes, every day. Snowdrop the cat had mellowed, but was still a mixture of huge affection and severe disapproval! Thomas, the tom-cat, had taken Warkworth over, had been made a member of the Mothers' Union and frequently attended Church – dodging the sidesmen, to the delight of the children (of all ages!)   did the rounds of the pubs, and was in and out of all the shops, rapidly establishing himself as a local institution, if not as the squire.

At which point it may be appropriate to commemorate some of the feline members of the Duncan household, past and present, who stoutly maintained their presence amongst the dogs.

A Celebration of Cats Eternal

Dear Tom! He now in Timelessness abides,
who slept, in Church, upon the Bishop's Throne –
Episcopuss – and now with Saints confides.
Magnificent, alone yet not alone,
he smiles, upon his cloud-perch in the sky,
and claws the hair of heavenly passers-by.

Dear Big Black Puss! From darkness into Light,
who daily strewed our mat with headless mice.
You noble Puss! – to tease was your delight –
you gave your life for us in sacrifice
and, on the stair – to make us hold our breath –
set forth the Resurrection after death.

Dear Snowdrop! The eternal Feminine,
out-womaning all Woman, in the raw!
Supremely vain, capricious without sin,
so soft and loving, fierce in tooth and claw.
Once Love, in you, performed – to stunned surprise –
a healing miracle before our eyes.

Dear Cats Eternal – Puss in Paradise –
who daily disciplined our hearth and home,
establishing equality as price
for privilege *their* residence to roam:
Our thanks for showing what it is to *be*,
and teaching us our own humanity.

However, against this idyllic backdrop Tony was finding it difficult to find a sense of direction and suitable style in his writing. He thought the experience of writing books such as *The Lord of the Dance* and *The Sword in the Sun* that had been in some sense "received" – and certainly different – made it difficult to find his own voice again, despite his success with *The Fourth Dimension*.

He sent me, and also to one or two other trusted friends, a semi-autobiographical manuscript called *Confessions of a Gregarious Hermit*. It took off from personal mystical experiences that led him to leave the army and join the church, along with interesting speculations, teaching and so on. But although it seemed a good formula in principle, I felt a little uneasy as to its application in practice. For instance, in the first chapter one soon got the impression that one was being talked to by a vicar, looking back with the benefit of hindsight. There was not enough of the raw experience of "the boozy young subaltern" and the immediacy of the holy awe of what he went through. It soon became conceptualised into "communion of saints", "death and resurrection", "transportation into the whole other". He and I might well know what he meant, but I bet the subaltern didn't – or the readers in most need of help either. Admittedly it was not an easy task, but I suggested that what he should be aiming at in such a book was the stark confrontation with mystical and spiritual, even psychic, experience – and then the coming to terms with it, the naturalness of it, the uniqueness of it, the paradoxes of spiritual and earthly coming together.

The fact was, and I think possibly remained, that it was in his poetry that he came closest to what his life was all about.

A Visitation

Two points of unexpected, living light,
the darkness all surrounding. Presences
suggesting form to my bewildered sight,
yet standing off from me as heralds
of some greater dawn. Dawn broke;
a man-shape, darker than the darkness, stood,
whose Uncreated Light my senses burned,
and while Creation shook, one Word He spoke.

Through that Humanity, an open door, I pass
uncomprehending now these sixteen years,
still questing: to interpret and obey.
The Quest is the obedience perhaps, for time
interprets timelessness imperfectly, in part,
and yearns for integration, mind in heart.

AT DEAD OF NIGHT

At dead of night, a summer night,
Great Love to little human love broke in
and brought the Resurrection to the crucified.

At dead of night, a shaft of light
shone slanting down; contained therein
a Host of Heaven and The Crucified.

At dead of night, so Heaven-bright.
The Peace was given and our hearts within
their context set, and glorified.

TO THE GUARDIAN ANGEL

Ours is a hidden comradeship of flesh and flame,
yet our embrace knows neither burn nor flare.
With you alone, who know my all, I know no shame
nor can I stand complaining to the empty air
while you reveal my self, with neither praise nor blame,
to me, who have but consequence to bear.

You are a liberation to me, and you stand
for Him who sent you ever by my side
and point the way, yet never stay my foolish hand
but often lightly lead along my pride
until its bubble bursts, and ever understand,
and make me understand your task, my guide.

There are no words of thanks, for you and I accept
each other's part within a common task;
for its fulfilment is our Joy, and while I'm kept
in this incarnate life I work, and ask
and find that you have led me on, and that I've leapt
and, from the Face of Heaven, plucked the mask.

A Glimpse of Reality

The prayer of ecstasy is done.
Those times are past and now, the soul abiding,
its mind within its heart, is one;
endures a gentler chiding,
its will now with the Will of God deciding.

This life is scarce begun.
Still young the soul, still fearful of backsliding
yet knows it is forever won,
within that Heart residing;
the Everlasting love ever confiding.

A new normality is this.
Simplicity of Love forever knowing;
its prayer as simple as a kiss
upon all things bestowing;
kiss on the hands, then sent to Heaven blowing.

Forgetfulness is bliss.
The self quite lost, the love of God bestowing;
and all in God is this.
Whose energies are flowing,
fulfilled within the joy of the unknowing.

Anyway, for what it was worth, he thanked me for my comments, and said what a head clearing thing my letter had been. It said exactly what he needed to hear, and it had been a great help to have things spelled out so lucidly. So it was back to the drawing board, and having articulated things theologically to try to say them differently and be a great deal clearer as to whom he was addressing.

Warkworth made writing possible – or at least a lot more possible, and he was two thirds of the way through a children's (or children's parents') book which gave him a lot of fun and would make an amusing second string to his bow if it worked. He had joined the Society of Authors and was looking for a literary agent with a view to becoming more professional about the business of writing.

But he later wrote to say that on the book writing front he continued to find himself butting up against a brick wall. All the agents said the same thing: "Hard times, great difficulties, severe economic pressures, etc" although they said it nicely on the whole!

Edward England, former religious publishing director for Hodders, had become a literary agent for religious writers, and said much the same thing. He was happy to describe Tony's stuff as "Good middle-of-the-road Anglican", which was just what nobody could afford to touch, although he was kind enough to say he thought it a temporary state of affairs. He suggested having a go at books of prayer rather than books *about* prayer. *Parish Prayers* and similar books went into reprint after reprint.

Tony's first reaction was "Ugh!" but it did occur to him that the man might well be right. He reasoned that folk are moulded by the prayers they say – and most folk <u>say</u> them – and thought he could do this quite well, but was somewhat torn between reluctance and temptation. And it seems that reluctance won.

At the end of the year the situation was much the same, he was plugging away submitting manuscripts to the most likely publishers and agents, playing, as he said, "a kind of literary Royal Tennis" with manuscripts, that is, bouncing them off the walls as well as off the floor! He had lots of encouraging rejection slips. Hodders bewailed the fact that his work did not fit neatly into any of the recognised categories of "Christian Books". At the moment Alick Bartholomew at Turnstone had had a manuscript for a month, which might be a hopeful sign, unless he was ski-ing in Switzerland!

However, having just returned from a retreat at Nashdom Abbey he was fired with a new approach to the same old vision. He would have to do some trial runs but was concerned to go some little way beyond *The Lord of the Dance* and its basic vision – which had been opening out quite some over the last few years – and drawing together into it both Teilhard de Chardin's later notions along with very good classical but little appreciated Eastern Orthodox thinking. All in a non-stuffy style. If he could make it read more like a detective story than a theological textbook then he might have got it about right. In fact it positively must *not* read like a theological textbook! He had a working title – *In Pursuit of a Vision* – and wondered that if he could justify a naked lady on the dust jacket, who knows, it might even sell!

Something of his sense of frustration at this time is summed up in the following verses:

A Prophet's Reward

If they will hear, or if they will forbear,
"No matter!" These long years my season's out;
I mouth my message to the empty air
but am not heard. The world, it goes about;
and I? I wrestle nightly with despair.

In season? Out of season evermore?
No matter! I must write down what I see
though none may read. Each like the one before
unread, unheard-of and unpublished. Me?
I stand before a never-opened door.

The hearing and the reading; they will come
or not come. And no matter! I must still
articulate, although as good as dumb,
what clamours from beyond me with a will
inexorable, though it leave me numb.

Mine, of a universal human mind
is but a part, inseparable. Now
I see. The whole shall see it all, and find
the truths of Truth in it. I care not how.
My present martyrdom is not unkind.

Or on a slightly lighter note:

An Absurdity

Were my poor pen to rise one day in fame,
myself long dead, that seems to be the rule,
my ancient but quite unscholastic name
would haunt the wretched pupil at his school.

Then would, on *Duncan*, students take degrees
between their pub-crawls, and the bright would reach
to Doctorates! And Fellows at their ease –
all things preposterous – would *Duncan* teach!

Duncan Symposia should then take place;
authorities on *Duncan* would appear,
and critical biographies apace
win scholars reputations by the year.

Though all shall earn immensely more than me,
still I prefer to, simply, *Duncan* be!

It cannot have been easy for him in this period, as somewhat ironically, things were burgeoning quite remarkably for me. It all began with an invitation to put on a weekend of lectures at Hawkwood in 1979, similar to his own engagement back in 1973 with its rather remarkable consequences, after he had responded to "the Archdeacon of Cheltenham's idea that I might be interested in doing something for that chap who runs Hawkwood and all his funny friends...!"

I chose to base my weekend on the Tree of Life of the Qabalah and it turned out to be a great success, all the more remarkable in that I covered much the same ground that Anthony Duncan had done back in 1973, and before a similar audience, including a number who had found his talk so disturbing. Things had obviously moved on a bit over the subsequent six years.

I followed up with further Hawkwood workshops through the rest of the next decade, now almost legendary for breaking new grounds in techniques of responsible magical working in public, some of them bringing books their wake; *The Secret Tradition in Arthurian Legend* in 1983, *The Rose Cross and the Goddess* in 1985, *The Treasure House of Images* (on the Tarot) in 1986 and *The Magical World of the Inklings* in 1991.

Despite the very positive experience Tony had had with esoteric conferences back on Iona ten years before, he no longer felt at ease with the Conference scene as it had since developed, and fancied he would not be asked again. The conference organisers were far from being Christocentric and regarded the Christian as just another way among many ways – the others being the more interesting because the more psychic and less apparently familiar. Despite going on like crazy about "incarnations", he doubted very much if they could quite cope with *The Incarnation*! "They obviously gagged a bit at the idea of a real Incarnation! Cosmic Christ and all that – but a *real* Incarnation? Jesus of Nazareth *not* an avatar like the Buddha etc.?" What also maddened him was the inability of some clergy to cope with the Cosmic Christ, that made him occasionally wonder if they had ever read the New Testament!

Meanwhile he was still becalmed, and with a sense of fidget about it, as he hated being becalmed, even if he knew it was healthy and necessary. But something had moved him to type out all his extant poetry, and in the process he was discovering a great deal in it that he had not realised before, as well as being somewhat astonished by the sheer volume.

In April 1981 he wrote to say that a great stillness had descended upon his literary activities. Various manuscripts had rushed round and round the countryside attracting the nicest possible rejection slips – all bewailing the recession in eloquent terms and hoping for jam tomorrow etc. In some strange way this did not worry him and he had eased off and given publishers and the Post Office a break for a bit. He felt that all the literary odds and ends of his would find their outlet some day, in some manner, and it did not seem his place to fret too much about how or when – at any rate for the moment.

He found himself waiting, reasonably patiently at last, for an indication of the next initiative. That there would be one, he had no doubt, but what it would be and in what direction he had no idea. And it was quite fun to be entirely without a clue what to do next or in which direction. He was inwardly assured that this was the right way to be, and relieved too not to feel too much inclined to put pen to paper, partly because of a growing conviction that "I don't know anything anyway!" So he waited to see what transpired, and hoped it would not take too long in the transpiring.

But a lot was going on inside. He was writing the odd magazine article to keep his hand in, and after meeting the editor of *New Fire*, the journal of the Cowley Fathers,[6] it seemed they were keen to encourage him. The readership was possibly 50% clerical but the articles they wanted from him seemed such as might appeal to someone like me!

Oddly enough, he had sensed some kind of Arthurian dynamic at the time of my 1981 Hawkwood workshop on the Arthurian legend, which had turned out to be an extremely powerful one that seemed to touch deep levels in the group soul of the nation.[7] He wrote to say

---

6 Familiar name for The Society of St John the Evangelist, an Anglican religious order for men founded at Oxford in 1866.
7 Details of the event are in my esoteric autobiography *I Called it Magic* (Skylight Press 2011)

he was fascinated by "the Arthurian thing" and without the slightest prompting, his meditational exercises had taken on a decidedly Arthurian character and clothing. A poem of his records something of this:

LOGRES

They came and took me by the hand
and led me down what winding stair,
deep down and deeper down,
until a cavern opened wide
where one sat still upon a chair;
upon his head a crown.

Into the dark on either hand
men lay as dead upon the floor.
I gazed upon the King
as on a waxwork, or upon
a scarecrow stuffed with straw;
a dead, neglected thing.

A chest stood at the King's right hand –
shrine-canopy in fragments broke –
all empty, opened wide.
I picked the pieces, made it new,
but all was silence, no man spoke;
nothing was found inside.

Then they that took me by the hand
said: "This is Logres; the within
that undergirdeth all
that you call England. Understand:
must each in Love the other win
or both together fall."

A sense of rejuvenation came to him as a result of a visit back to Gloucestershire in May 1981. (Hard on my Arthurian workshop as it happened!)

> We have just returned from a wonderful holiday in Gloucestershire. It did nothing for our figures but everything for morale. By the most extraordinary set of circumstances I have returned to every church where I have been Curate, Vicar or Rector in the last three weeks or so. Two Sundays ago I was at Tewkesbury Abbey, not long before that at Parkend, and the first Sunday of our holiday we went to Highnam in the morning and Rudford (the parish that goes with it) in the afternoon. And immediately on our return we found ourselves at St. John's for the very first time since I left two and a half years ago. It all seemed to be a "significant" but by no means intended pilgrimage. I have a great sense of having "finished" on one hand (or plane, or level – or something) and "starting" on another. This feeling has been with me for quite a while and the holiday seemed to emphasise it mightily.

He also remarked that while he was sitting in the church at Highnam on this occasion, he realised that the three and a half years he had spent there were, on every level, among the most "significant" of his life so far. At the moment he realised that he had had to withdraw from one thing after another and learn to close down level after level in which he had become, inevitably, far too open. Whilst under it all a vast sorting out process had been going on. He hoped it was in the progression: Knowledge – Understanding – (one day) – Wisdom, and that he might actually be able to do something useful with all the "training" of the last umpteen years. But he was not convinced that he was called to put a sign out (or an advert in the village Post Office) saying "*A.D. Duncan, Guru*".

But the Lord was ever full of surprises, and it might be that He was (or had been) waiting for his many "openings" to close up and a multitude of sensitivities to come under a higher level of control (*he wondered what he meant by that, but thought he did!*) and for the wine within to stop fermenting and become drinkable. Then, in His own good time the Almighty might unwire the cork and he would know what he was supposed to be doing, both in principle and detail. Meanwhile, life was far from dull, and with regard to my current operations at Hawkwood he was glad to think that the event at that Palm Sunday weekend all those years ago (1973) had been fruitful. It had been quite an occasion about which he retained pleasant memories.

Evidence of a new initiative came from him in September with a letter saying he had been writing poetry with a very full head of steam in recent weeks. And that he was intending to publish it himself, as nobody else was likely to! He asked my advice about obtaining an ISBN and the technicalities of setting up an imprint, which he duly did, as Parvis Books, Warkworth, for the publication of *The Lover Within*.

It was a collection of 28 devotional poems plus a dedication to the Virgin Mary, and very much influenced I think by his recent reading of the *Classics of Christian Mysticism* and the encouragement from the Cowley Fathers. A sample follows:

THE LOVER WITHIN

I sought my Lord. I ran about the town
in search of him, asked this one after that
for news of him, knocked at each house and flat,
sent messengers abroad, paced up and down
and called, and called; threw up the windows wide
and gazed into the foggy dark, then turned
and looked about me for a lamp that burned
enough to penetrate the fog outside.

How many years? How long a pilgrimage
to shrines and tabernacles here and there?
How long a floundering, of mortal sin
afraid, afraid? Until the privilege
unutterable dawned, and called through my despair:
"Your Lover whom you seek is here, within!"

"OF THE EARTH, EARTHY"

I hope for Heaven, but I go astray
on hates and heresies which rob the soul
of flesh and blood; which will not have me whole
but only spiritual; make me betray
the Incarnation; go some other way.
Earth is my Heaven now! I will extol
her. Earth is given to me to control –
I am the Steward, these his goods – today!

I hope for Heaven. My Paradise is now;
my Purgatory too. I'll have it whole,
now and hereafter, unbeset by fears.
This present earthly moment shall allow
the Earth's transfiguration, pole to pole,
for Christ's own dusty feet were washed with tears.

My Neighbour

Who is my neighbour? I am bound to see
my lord in him, to serve and to adore.
The principle I know; the practice sore
betrays me for I cannot chose to be
neighbour to whom I will. Humanity
is one. The very man whom I abhor
the most is Christ no less. And Christ's own law:
"Love one another," makes a knave of me.

It is not possible. My lord alone
can love and take me with him, change my sight.
I am my own first neighbour. He loves me
and heals the hates of self which I have thrown
broadcast upon my fellow-men; gives light
to heal my inner darkness; sets me free.

The Image of God

I make an image of my Lord and God
and worship it. From my disordered mind
projections flow. I build a shell, and proud,
unsatisfactory energies, and odd
dynamics fill it up, and I am blind
and deaf to truth. No golden calves allowed!

The living image of my Lord and God
was born and walked the Earth, and loved, and died;
and conquering death, all human life endowed.
Anthropomorphic image this, most odd

that Truth should turn out thus, by God supplied.
God in a man! No golden calves allowed!

I am the image of my Lord and God.
Imagination and creative mind
are given me. Thoughts and creations crowd
within and manifest without. A nod
will set me off again to make, to find,
give life, and love. No golden calves allowed!

The Monastery

I am a monk, and called to play my part
in life doing the Work of God
in prayer's unceasing round.
On this my path, well marked, well trod,
dangers enough abound.
As through the world, a monk, I plod,
my monastery abides within my heart.

I am a hermit, and I live apart
the better to embrace them all,
my God and man in prayer.
Such is my nature, such my call.
And so, abiding there,
I tramp the world; and lest I fall
I wear my hermitage within my heart.

Mine is a Highland croft, and I would start
there now and, under a great Ben,
live out a simple life.
But I am called to leave the glen
to live in worldly strife.
That I may serve my fellow-men,
my croft abides there yet, within my heart.

To the Mother of God

Dear Lady, hierarch of the human race;
accept as if a bunch of flowers
from Earth, to be arranged in Heaven's height
and set before the Father's face,
these stumbling lines; the best that my poor powers
can yet contrive, or pen can write.

Mother of God; I mind you once did lace
your favour to my helm; the hours
to sing, to offer as a priest, to fight.
Pray for me, Lady, that by grace
I shall win through and come into your bowers,
and of your Son may have full sight.

Their writing is obviously a personal statement of where he stands and what he believes and seems intended for his own kind (he was an oblate of the Benedictine order) rather than for the wider public (not that the wider public would not benefit enormously by taking them to heart!) He probably sent a copy of them to a fellow poet and religious, as suggested by some lines in memory of her.

Sister

When you had died they tidied up your things
and worked through your address book, letting know
how Sister did that kind of thing and later on did this;
how Sister died a holy death. Those fine grey eyes,
fulfilled their Faith, shine brighter under fairer skies.

We flew, the pair of us, on kindred wings;
your sonnets, thoughtful, finely turned to show
an ordered mind, compassionate. Nor did you miss
the chance to praise, encourage and review
most kindly the "slim volume" I, misgiving, sent to you!

How diffident the scribbler who has a heart that sings;
wide open, vulnerable to comment that can blow
all confidence apart! And so how ready to dismiss
a kindred spirit, make his strivings sound absurd!
Not you my dear. You set me free. Rest kindly in the Word.

At much the same time that all this was going on he announced that he and Helga, as well as celebrating their silver wedding, had taken up middle aged mountaineering! And lest I should think he was waxing symbolical – "Exoteric, external mountains by the way! Things like Scafell Pike, Helvelyn and Skiddaw." And there were poems to prove it.

Helvelyn

Gaunt, grey and gleaming and the last cliff climbed;
three thousand feet, above the everlasting cloud
eternal, ever-spreading, to the presence of a lamb,
content and sandwich-foraging. A pilgrimage is this
into the blue, the brilliance of this high-hued heaven.

A rocky islet ragged in a sea celestial,
all pilgrim-peopled, swirling, smiling out the mist
to pause awhile and vanish. All the stridings on the edge,
the strivings, gropings fearfully, all far away, forgot
for all is now and clarity. Reality, this spot.

Now comes the stirring and the fitful, faithful plunge
down, down to damp and dimness, an eroded track,
slipping and jolting down the long trek back,
yet streaming trails of glory. Sustaining an elation
to motor-car and mud and rain; a former incarnation!

And more than a hint of the purpose of their being there.

The Priesthood of Man

Water running over stone,
heather blowing in the breeze,
silent tree and fallen cone,
summer sun and winter freeze,

signs and symbols in each place,
touchstones deep within the heart,
all are Nature's means of Grace
for the souls called, set apart

to articulate the hills,
set the land to dance and song;
feel its archetypal thrills,
bear its burdens all along.

So must Man and Woman be
priest and priestess to each place;
thus the very Earth shall see
made and Maker, face to Face.

They had also moved house, if only three doors up the street, but an astonishing three day move by wheelbarrow, horsebox, tractor and a rather "fragrant" farm trailer. The new vicarage was in fact two hundred years older than the old vicarage, but a vast improvement on anything they had had before. It took a great deal of stress and strain out of life to be living somewhere "normal" – that is to say, that included indoor "facilities".

1982 proved to be a busy year all round, including a further venture into broadcasting when he did three sessions on *Prayer for the Day*, after which the fan mail had been very appreciative save for one magnificent letter from a lady in Keswick who eventually conceded that his talk was obviously *"well-meant!"* He was glad she thought so.

This was also the year when I wound up Helios Book Service Publications and gave any remaining stock to the various authors. This concerned *The Lord of the Dance* and *The Christ, Psychotherapy &*

Magic as far as Tony Duncan was concerned, which he was happy to display alongside Parvis Books on the church bookstall, from whence they continued to sell about 15 to 20 copies a year.

Parvis had also published a second book of poems with five contributors including himself, funded by subscription and a grant from the local Arts Council, all in aid of Alwinton Church in the Cheviots. This included a poetry reading in July and he found it fun to publish what local poets would be reading, and was happy to devote the proceeds to charity. As I had found myself, doing one's own publishing, although small beer compared to large commercial concerns, had its own rewards. And, as I had found, could, in a specialist field, even be quite profitable – although perhaps not sufficient to stock the refrigerator or pay the mortgage!

They had both also discovered watercolour painting, in which Helga proved a "natural" and after picking up a brush for the first time had already sold three paintings, with commissions for more, and won an enormous silver cup as first prize at the local Horticultural Show ("Industrial Section"). Even Tony had sold a painting, the first one he ever did!

He was glad to hear that, after my visiting Tewkesbury Abbey and finding one of the holiest places in the building, a former hermit's cell, changed from Chapel of the Holy Cross to broom cupboard, I had, as a Life Member of the Friends of Tewkesbury Abbey, posted a polite note of protest in the charity box, attached to a ten pound note, and the *status quo ante* had been restored. He thought it was perhaps due to a new vicar who, in his eyes, appeared to be a very good number indeed.

So things rested, without much communication between us, until October 1984 when I paid him a visit which we both found enjoyable and not unimportant. As he remarked, "it is good to meet others who are battling on a nearby sector of the same front and who share the same radio-net, codebook, NAAFI, or what you will. One simply cannot talk about these things other than to those likewise involved."

I had been quite grabbed by a one-creature-infinitude-of-persons doctrine that had seemed to him, when he first encountered it, a blinding glimpse of the obvious, although as he said, its implications – and the implications of real belief in the Incarnation – were cosmic dynamite!

Apart from that, we shared views on our contributions to a popular Newsletter on the Esoteric Conference circuit, which as he later put it, tended to cater for "a great mish-mash of sweetness, light, wholefood, meditation, long-hair, bare-feet, dressed-in-old-curtains – you know the scene. With some very sensible and good folk in the middle of the 'meditation on social security' (or Daddy's money)." True enough, so far as it went, but one had to bear in mind C.S.Lewis' warning in *The Screwtape Letters* about being put off by the unprepossessing aspect of some members of church congregations!

One of his articles, which covered much the same points as mentioned above, made use of a popular cartoon strip to compare humanity (or Adam and Eve) to the highly dysfunctional marriage of Andy Capp and Flo.

THY WILL BE DONE? YOU MUST BE JOKING!

Of course we all know what to do. It is very simple, really. Lao-tse figured it out and expressed it beautifully. The whole Cosmos is in a wonderful harmony and order. All, that is, except Man. Now if Man would only observe, and then do likewise, wouldn't it be lovely? Full marks, Lao-tse, I love your teaching dearly. Trouble is – we just don't seem to do it that's all.

Confucius, he say … and he was so right. If we just did what Confucius, he say, everything in the garden would be roses. And Buddha too. I couldn't agree more with the Four Noble Truths and the Eightfold Path. Trouble is, I seem to have problems actually doing it. I have the best of intentions, believe me. But somehow…something ain't right. It is all the fault of Andy Capp and Flo. They did what they didn't oughter. They ate apples and things. Well the strip-cartoon was called Adam and Eve as it happened, but the principle is the same. In the context of an end-of-the-page giggle it was saying something profound. We identify with the strip-cartoon characters. It is *us* really.

The names are clever too. Adam means Mankind; (the word is derived from "the dust of the earth"), Eve means "life". Everyman and his Missus on one level, "Man" the articulate, reasoning, freely-choosing creature on another level. Either way, he started pinching from the till and got the sack. He has been on the fiddle, congenitally crooked ever since. That would have made sense to Lao-Tse. Confucius, maybe he say, probably he think… And I fancy Buddha would have nodded gravely and smiled a sad, enigmatic smile.

Mention the word "doctrine" and people switch off. Well, switch back on again because this is fundamental. There is only ONE creature – Man. Mankind is ONE. Mankind images the Creator (how could he do otherwise?) in that he/she is ONE creature with an infinitude of Persons, each of infinite and eternal value, but the integrity of the Many is bound up with the integrity of the ONE. How does this image the Creator? The Christian understanding of – and experience of – God is of the Holy Trinity; One God – Three Persons, co-equal, co-eternal. Now this is a mystery and quite beyond our understanding. We believe it to be of Revelation; it may be in some sense *known* but it cannot be in any real sense known *about*. "God is Love" says St. John. The Doctrine of the Trinity says "God is a Love Affair". Man is a Love Affair. Yes, but somehow…Belsen. The Dresden Fire Raid. Hiroshima. The Rape of Nankin. Vietnam. Bullying in the school yard. Torture. Nagging. Greed. Power-seeking. Sex-grabbing. Mankind is a Love Affair for all that, but it goes wrong, over and over again. I go wrong all the time. If you will allow the suggestion, most respectable reader, so do you.

Why can't we be OPEN in the right action, thought, feeling, in the Context of the Wellbeing of the Whole? 'Cos we are sinners, that's why. Andy Capp and all that. "I cannot understand my own behaviour," says St. Paul. "I fail to carry out the things I want to do, and I find myself doing the very things I hate…In fact, this seems to be the rule, that every single time I want to do good it is something evil that comes to hand. In my inmost self I dearly love God's Law, but I can see that my body follows a different law that battles against the law which my reason dictates. This is what makes me a prisoner...What a wretched man I am! Who will rescue me from this body doomed to death? Thanks be to God through Jesus Christ our Lord!"

Christians believe, not in avatars or incarnations, but in The Incarnation. "The Word became flesh and dwelt among us" as a Person of that One Creature, Mankind. The integrity of the one and the many – and the ONE – are all bound up inextricably. Mankind is a Love Affair, like God; so they blackguarded Him, lashed the flesh off His back and choked Him to death by nailing Him to two bits of wood. It was a triumph of Love, and Mankind can never be the same again. We have hardly *begun* to think of the implications of The Incarnation for Mankind. It is easier to waffle on about theology, or "incarnations" or vague "cosmics" of one sort and another, while Godhead lies, like a time-bomb in our midst.

"Thy Will be done?" You must be joking! It is as hard as ever it was. Only by heroic effort, aided by Grace, can we begin to acquire the habit of wanting to want God, and wanting to want the Will of God to be done. The Incarnation was not into plaster sainthood but into a hell of a mess. It is from within the context of the hell of a mess that we are called, enabled, into a new, a "wholly other" *becoming*. It is all a matter of Faith of course. But we have sure and certain Hope. And the name of the game is LOVE.

In the context of his remarks in the article about some of the iniquities of the Second World War, the following poem raises a point that no doubt bore heavily on Tony and Helga when they proposed to marry – representatives of different sides capable of inhuman horrors in the recent conflict.

AUSCHWITZ AND DRESDEN

Declare a race inhuman and the heart
of him declaring dies. The monstrous mind,
inhuman, with its world twisted apart,
destroys itself, destroying its own kind.

To demonise, in war, a total folk
is to become demonic. Such a mind,
with lunatic self-righteous wrath to choke
all right or reason, slaughters its own kind.

The vanquished must the monstrous mirror face
and come to terms with what they find therein.
Not so the new, victorious Master Race
Which fades in unfaced and unshriven sin.

One does the psychopath the more deprave;
One prostitutes the bravery of the brave.

He had come across a book of mine about "the Feminine thing", as he put it, which he thought said some very important things and rang familiar and urgent bells for him. This would have been *The Rose Cross and the Goddess*,[8] deriving from my 1982 and 1983 Hawkwood workshops. With examples from ancient Greece, the Graeco-Roman world, 17th century Rosicrucian spiritual alchemy, Tibetan Mahayana Buddhism and an analysis of the legendary origins of the cult of the Virgin, I had striven to show how coming to terms with the Eternal Feminine principle was an urgent need for modern mankind, whose psychic unbalance threatened to destroy life on the planet.

He was sorry to see that it had got a "completely missed the point" review in *New Fire*. "Alas! Sadly predictable if the reviewer loses sight of point number one: 'to whom is it addressed?' He did! But I too got a 'completely missed the point' review in *Church Times*, so in this as in other things we have things in common!"

This *Church Times* review may have referred to a new book of his own that came out in 1986 – *Jesus Essential Readings*. He had been commissioned to edit an anthology of sayings attributed to Jesus. It came out under the Crucible imprint, which was part of Aquarian Press, a long standing esoteric publisher (and at that time publisher of my own books) who were apparently finding a Christian line quite within their remit as an alternative to the established rather "churchy" religious publishing houses.

He rose magnificently to the occasion. The book was reprinted within six months, taken up by a book club, and translation rights sold. At which point he yelled to Helga as he opened one letter, "Darling! I've got Portuguese Rights!" Who not untypically responded "Good God! Is that like Aids or something?"

---

[8] An expanded revised edition was published by Destiny Books in the USA retitled *Evoking the Goddess* in 1983 and again as *Magic and the Power of the Goddess* in 2008.

The project was of particular interest to me, as in the occult school where I had received my esoteric training it had been recommended that concentration upon actual sayings of Jesus recorded in the Gospels could be a very useful exercise. And I had at one time gone through a New English Bible underlining such phrases in red. Not so simple a task as it may sound, as a matter of fact.

Tony Duncan's approach was more well informed I have to say, with the benefit of his Bible studies and theological training. He provided a helpful introduction outlining the development of the four Gospels and the sources from which they were compiled, grouping the teachings under thematic headings, each with an introductory essay. And he also took into his remit various Apocryphal sources, such as the *Gospel of Thomas*, and the *Apocryphon of James*, recently come to light as a result of the Nag Hammadi manuscript discoveries.

As for the book itself, as he said in his introductory paragraphs:

> We shall be encountering the words – the reported words – of a young man of whom, historically, remarkably little is known, who never wrote down a word for posterity, and who was dishonestly "got rid of" by the authorities on a trumped-up charge, as a politico-religious nuisance, in his mid-thirties. And all of that a very long time ago.

Yet by the same token an event that had cosmic implications:

> The *experience of Jesus*, however, caused his followers to claim what they have continued to claim for almost two thousand years, namely: "God was, in Christ, reconciling the world to himself."

Whatever one chooses to make of the Resurrection, I recall Tony Duncan remarking that there seemed no question of being an "astral body" as some esoteric enthusiasts liked to assume, insofar that when he appeared before the astonished disciples he joined them in a meal of fish and chips! (Well perhaps not the chips – but certainly the fish was mentioned.)

Another Apocryphal fragment, which concluded the book, was *The Hymn of Jesus*. I found this particularly interesting for I had come across it before in my esoteric studies. He described it as follows:

> The ecstatic dance has long been a part of the Jewish religious tradition and ecstatics have always featured in Israel. There need be nothing odd

about the idea of the Last Supper ending in a dance, despite the almost board-room solemnity that Western Christians have invested it with. St Matthew's Gospel tells us that "When they had sung a hymn, they went out to the Mount of Olives". Here, we are invited to believe, is that hymn!

St John, as reported in *The Acts of John,* tells us that Jesus said: "Before I am delivered to them, let us sing a hymn to the Father, and so go to meet what lies before us." So he told us to form a circle, holding one another's hands, and himself stood in the middle and said, "Answer 'Amen' to me." So Jesus began to sing the hymn and to say:

Glory be to thee, Father [and we circled round him and answered him]
                                                            Amen.
Glory be to thee, Logos   Amen.
Glory be to thee O Grace   Amen.

And so it goes on for a considerable number of more lines, which does not look all that impressive upon the page. However, I had experienced performing it in a magical context (that is to say raising consciousness by means of an "acted out" form of meditation) when working with the occultist W.G.Gray back in 1965. The technique is to make each of the rubrics seven syllables long, as also the responses, thus: "*Ah – ah – ah – ah – ah – ah – men.*" To do this, circling round and round for some time, as a rhythm and mood builds up, and then to be suddenly stopped in one's tracks by the leader commanding:

"Be still! And know the One I Am."

The depth of silence and stillness that ensues is profound, and what I am sure Tony Duncan would have defined as being upon the threshold of mystical contemplation.

In the version given in the *Acts of John* a similar kind of action and result must have been experienced, as it concludes:

> After the Lord had so danced with us, my beloved, he went out. And we were like men amazed or fast asleep, and we fled this way and that.

However, back in the modern world things were also radically changing. At the end of 1986 the local Bishop offered Tony a new job as Hospital Chaplain at Hexham, together with a tiny country parish of Whitley Chapel with a paradisal vicarage.

7

WHITLEY MILL

At Whitley Mill Tony Duncan was much taken with the fact that one of his titles was "Vicar of the Shire". The inhabitants of the parish called themselves "Shire Folk", not that many of them had probably read Tolkien.

Hexhamshire was an ancient "peculiar" in Anglican administrative terms, as it came directly under the Archbishop of York rather than the local bishop. Part of it once went with Hexham Abbey until it became a parish in 1762, when what Tony Duncan referred to as "a beautiful toy church" was built on a site "of desperate antiquity". In this toy church he was destined to play vicar – which he thought huge fun.

The vicarage turned out to be a dream-house, 500 ft above sea-level on a south facing slope with a small river running through the garden. An eight-acre glebe field adjoined the garden, and a hanging wood with deer roaming in it, that also contained a badger sett. A wonderful part of the world he thought, and almost completely unknown, even in Northumberland, five miles south of Hexham. The parish was bounded by fell tops and rivers, where "all roads petered out!" It was a place and situation that Tony Duncan thought would prove ideal. Enough to do and to stimulate, but not too much. Plenty of physical work in the garden, with time and space to think, pray and write.

In other words, a true country parson set-up, and not one of those "five-church-nonsenses" that set a country parson running as fast as a town one but with fewer resources. He was well pleased and thankful and a later bucolic poem tells in retrospect, something of the ambience of Whitley Mill.

Whitley Vicarage

Works that grey heron yet the Rowley Burn?
And stands he still stock-still beneath the bridge?
And yet do ash and alder haste to hide,
in height and hedge along the banks beside,
all goods and gardens from the Vicarage?

Yet runs the Rowley round the Glebe, to turn
and meet the Ham Burn's wild and wooded wind?
Still stay the badgers in their Glebe Wood sett?
And scramble yows across those dyke tops yet,
knowing and nimble, out of sight and mind?

Wade still the deer across the moonlit burn
to start and tremble at each whispered sound?
And, deep in silence of each silvered night,
dance yet the unseen elf and water sprite
their measure on that many-hallowed ground?

And an ingeniously compiled topographical poem recounts something of the Shire.

The Devil Water

First; Epsey Syke, through moss and field,
falls by the folds to Harwood Shield
where stands a milestone by the bridge.
Second: the syke from Beldon ridge
rough-tumbles all the Peat Hill down
to waters meet. The Steel Crags frown
on crowded bush and briar and tree.
Then joins the burn from Stobby Lea
to make one river of them all.
To South, above the waterfall,
far up on long north facing slope,
there stand the blind walls of Low Hope.
The Black Burn falls from Blackburn Head
to "Devil Water" name of dread,
which tumbles on within its trough
to widely wind round Burntshield Haugh.
Below Ead's Bush the flood declines
to Embley Bank and ancient mines.
By Kittybridge and Facey's Wood,
below where Renny's Barns have stood,
below where Viewley views far off,
past Quaker's Well and Ginglinghaugh,
the river broadens, deepens still
to Moss House and the Redlead Mill.
By Holly Well and ancient smelt,
beneath the road bridge at full pelt
into the gorge and running still
to Peth Foot, past Finechambers Mill,
the river runs; by Nunsbrough winds
and, winding still, the Linnels finds
and Linnels Bridge – thence to expire
beyond the bounds of Hexhamshire.

He had not been there long before I received a slim volume, that he said compelled itself to be compiled, and that he had typed up (with only two errors!), and photocopied to send out to a few friends. Its title, *Tangible Appearances,* was culled from the first line of the first poem in the book, which summed up both psychic and mystical levels of his experience of the world, with its ultimate basis of divine love.

Love Germinates

A world of tangible appearances
shot through and through with Presence;
and with presences that utter, inarticulate,
but echo in my inmost deeps;
all this, my life.

          Disturbances,
unwanted resonations making claims
ungrasped, ungroped-for, inchoate
yet reaching ever for the inmost heart.
While stirring, fitful, in the dust
of old bewilderments and fears,
yet watered thus, Love germinates.

Other poems looked back to various points in his life, such as the theological college he attended on leaving the army prior to his ordination at Tewkesbury.

Chichester: the Theological College

Doorway to heaven off the dusty street,
absurdities within. A wilderness of books;
a plaster Saint upon the staircase blessed
in puzzlement the laundry tumbling down.
Pious extravagance, unbridled mirth;
a place of unexpected corners, sharp,
with holy water as their grinding paste.
A monstrous head of froth upon the beer
of the One True Faith. Withal
a thrown-together time and all too short.
Too long, as each prepared for his own Day.
This brief, absurd monastic interlude
between the old life ended, life begun,
taught me to laugh, to think, to love, to pray.

Through to one that summed up the present pretty well, and his efforts over recent years at Warkworth to find a means of expressing himself in books, and looking forward in hope to the immediate future.

The Gardener

I grow in my own garden. The dark soil
delves deep in me and digs me true;
tugs at my tangled inner thorns
and battles down the briars within
and burns; lets light come flooding through.

I am new-planted now and watered deep
to draw down roots, to feed, to drink.
I put on stem and healthy leaf,
break out new buds, awake from sleep
of winter the most dire, all life review.

So may this tortured stock yet flower most fair,
yet bring forth fruit to harvest-home.
Thus is my garden my own gardener,
transforming bitter ashes into loam
fit for the planting, and my life made new.

It included a look back to the world of faery, such as he had first experienced at Highnam but had since moved on from in terms of immediate concern, realising that each world had its own business and destiny, and at the same time regretting what the human abuse of the planet might have done to the natural world.

Faerie

Spirits of wood and water, garden, field,
imposed a change of emphasis; a shift
most subtle into other realms.
Parameters receded, and a world
quite other than the one I knew
slipped half-unnoticed into mine,
invited me to walk the two between.

I gave the Peace. By other hands
was drawn into a fellowship, accepted,
loved and known. I wander still
nor yet enchanted, nor in search
of that half-glimpsed; but in my heart
a penitence abides for all my world has done;
the Vision Splendid that my world has torn apart.

Another poem also harked back to the past, recalling some of the occasional bracing climatic events in Gloucestershire that chimed with his own inner experience then as now.

Blackthorn Winter

Blackthorn winter is a sudden snow
between the Lambing and the Gosling Storms
(though unconnected with the Tulip Wind).
So is my memory reactivate
and intermeshed with wisdom past
and ever. Now uprooted long,
my roots take hold. Sap rises.

Between the Lambing and the Gosling Storms
my world awakes and bonfires burn.
Stockbrokers' Winter and the Bankers' Drought
make compost now. I am reborn,
reincarnated; and the blackthorn flowers,
its winter past. Yet I have sinned:
too occupied to mark, to feel the Tulip Wind.

Blackthorn winter: Cold dry winds during March and April.
Gosling storm: A sudden squall of rain or sleet.
Lambing storm: A slight fall of snow in the spring.
Tulip Wind: A late winter/early spring freezing wind.

He had recently come across and was reading (for the third time) a little book by Gordon Strachan called *Christ and the Cosmos*,[9] that, he said, showed what could happen when a more than usually open-minded Church of Scotland theologian took a sabbatical and discovered that the books he was reading, and the book he was writing, were not at all what he *thought* he was going to! (He knew the feeling!)

Dr Strachan's sabbatical had indeed led him into some unexpected lines of thought. In an almost apologetic preface he said he had intended to write something about the Bible's attitude to nature – "the Lord is my shepherd", "consider the lilies of the field" and such like, all pleasantly pastoral. But the more he studied the Bible the more he found himself looking *through* nature to the cosmos. And that nature, as understood by Biblical writers, was only the terrestrial part of a cosmology which embraced the whole universe, leading into such taboo subjects as numerology, sacred geometry and astrological astronomy.

He had not intended to get involved with such suspect disciplines and it upset him to have to do so, but Biblical cosmology was all about geometric proportions, cycles of the heavenly bodies, and numbers. It was the way in which Biblical writers viewed the universe, and that view affected their faith in God through a surprisingly sophisticated range of symbol, metaphor, analogy and philosophy. Over the centuries, much of this had been ignored or dangerously distorted, resulting in an inward looking, Church centred understanding of religion, rather than a Creation centred cosmic one.

Naturally this was music to Tony Duncan's ears, who had recently expressed his despair at the lack of realisation, bordering upon ignorance, of the cosmic side of the Christian vision. And from personal experience he could sympathise with Gordon Strachan finding himself presented with unexpected truths from unexpected sources.

In the meantime he contented himself with running off two more little booklets of poetry, *The Great Work* and *Life Goes A-Gathering*.

Life Goes A-Gathering was a collection of fifty poems, that took its title from a line in the last poem in the book. One which had its cosmic implications:

---

9 Later reissued with additional material by Floris Books in 2005 as *The Bible's Hidden Cosmology* along with further books by Gordon Strachan on like subjects.

LIFE

The work of years: it is the taking in
of things, their ever-presence in the mind.
And so with persons, each in each
interior, all living in the heart and head
contemporary, in this present world, or dead.

The past is present, living now, within;
the present rolling to embrace what it shall find.
Ever expanding, all within its reach,
life goes a-gathering and living where it's led
'till all is dared and ventured and all sayable is said.

It included an interesting couple of snapshots of his army life, in Germany and Malaysia.

DIE LÜNEBURGER HEIDE

My sleeping bag by every bush and tree
one time has lain; my tyre marks were traced
on every forest track. The unmade roads
the steeply cambered cobbles, curving high,
remember yet the times when I passed by.

Jeep-mounted, trailer bouncing, free
to pounce where I might please, platoon now placed
in forests, farmyards, or by remote abodes,
their owners patient, friendly for our stay;
made claims for compensation when we drove away.

I hunted for wild boar at night, illegally,
(but never by that fearsome foe was faced)
transcending law by all the curious codes
of occupying armies on that higher plane:
"White man and native!" I could not pretend again.

Toy-soldier time; writ large the nursery!
A young man's time, its memory defaced
by one or two. Self-seeking and ambition were their goads.
I learned to love in stumbling, compassion in each lurch;
I heard then more confessions than I've ever heard in Church!

In Seremban

Red candles flicker in an ancient tree
all festive hung with lanterns and with prayer,
joss-fragrant. Rooted in the here and now
a fresh-air barber clips beneath the bough.

The races and their several smells flip-flop about,
acknowledging. The main road pauses for a sacred cow.
Tuan and his *Mem* drive, starched and laundered by,
excluded from the greater part beneath this sky.

A common heritage exists for all to find.
Though *Orang Puteh* finds it not his place to try,
his *Amah* mumbles at the trunk to which were tied
the wartime prisoners. There, bayoneted, they died.

Though what moves whom is known only to God;
why and to whom devotion thus supplied.
Hantu perhaps, or spirit of the tree?
Propitiation? Or for luck with *Chap-Ji-Kee!*

Tuan & Mem = British Officer and his Wife.
Orang puteh = White Man.
Amah = Domestic Servant.
Hantu = Ghost.
Chap-Ji-Kee = Chinese Lottery.

The British officer and his wife "starched and laundered, excluded from the greater part beneath this sky!" like "white man and native" expressed even in West Germany are indications of his deep lying belief in the at-one-ment of humankind "transcending law by all the curious codes of occupying armies". An attitude that received scorching comment in a poem on the "Aldershot" mentality.

Aldershot

Expatriates, they live in Aldershot.
Theirs is a drinks and dinner social set,
forever meeting those already met;
maintaining standards, lest they be forgot.

The mystic Aldershot, it manifests
in mufti where once uniform was seen,
preserves the ambience of what has been
but is not and, confronted thus, protests.

For Aldershot's a bubble. Safe within,
and safe from contact with the world outside,
expatriates can live their lives, and hide
from harsh realities, and drink their gin.

The pass is sold and Aldershot is done
when chaps "go native" with the local folk,
learn languages, begin to see the joke
of being Aldershot in tropic sun.

A "safe bubble" mentality that would presumably also have some difficulty in coming to terms with Elemental kingdoms, also revisited in *Life Goes A-Gathering*!

Development

Spirits of wood and water, stone and field,
whom my sophistication disallows, yet bide
and creep beneath my carapace. I know you well;
when walking pass unspoken time of day,
am sympathetic to your care and cause
and in much urgent enterprise am given pause.

We fool ourselves! Our fate, not yours, is sealed
by haste and havoc. We have nowhere left to hide;
ploughed up is paradise and harrowed into hell.
Our human life is herded, overstuffed, turned grey,
secured against all silence. On our minds,
irrationally rationalist, are pulled the blinds.

But whatever his awareness of psychic or mystical states and beings, Anthony Duncan was above all a great lover and observer of his fellow human beings, which was one of the great strengths of his ministry and popularity with his parishioners. Illustrated by this charming vignette of a very human being at one of his former parishes.

Auntie

Long-legged, ranging, with a roman nose,
she led her ladies on their warpaths wild
to stand full foursquare, nostrils flared
as one inhaling smoke, exhaling flame,
and snorted. Harridan, she gazed about her, bleak;
then set about the garden where I'd worked all week.

The parish called her Auntie. Goodness knows
her origins! From Leicester likely, or a child
from out of Clun perhaps, but delve who dared.
The discipline of dogs was her great fame,
none dared to deviate
who glimpsed her gaze;
authority her aura all her daunting days.

A termagant was she; as soon would eat a rose
as scent it! A virago, but with manner mild,
disarming almost. For her little ones she spared
no efforts; reared in villainy! And not the same
the Forest now she's dead and gone, which trembled at her will.
I loved her all those years ago. I love her still.

The Great Work, on the other hand was a shorter collection of poems expressing some of his doubts about the esoteric views and practices in our early discussions, some of which we have quoted in the Parkend years. Others showed that he was less than impressed by contemporary efforts to colonise the cosmos.

Crying for the Moon

So man has landed, walked upon the moon
and motored, briefly, in a little car,
dug up some dirt and rocks, such as there are,
and made it back – and not a mite too soon.

The style? That of a seaside holiday;
beach-buggying and digging in the sand –
this time upon the driest of dry land –
searching the while for Life flown far away,

if Life indeed there was. What do we mean
by what we look for, out in outer space?
Approximations of the human race
to whom we can relate? To whom our scene

of star-wars, laser-guns and sudden death
comes second nature, and with whom we'll play
at cops and robbers 'till the Judgement Day?
We've got it wrong. We waste our time and breath.

We're looking at these worlds from where we stand
and as we are; a life of loneliness
locked up in Time within a timelessness
we – sort of – used to know, half-understand.

Our explorations are upon one plane,
dimension, wavelength – call it what you will –
and our technology abides there still.
Rockets, and moons, and space, they all remain

for us upon that level of them where
we ontologically now abide
(if that's the word). For us to get inside
or up above is more than we could bear.

For, though I doubt it, if our rockets could
transcend dimensions, move between the planes,
and there encounter Life – would there be gains?
How to relate to Alien – or Good?

His recent burst of poetry had apparently been stimulated by a fortnight back in Gloucestershire, much of it in Tewkesbury. One of those times, he said, when a holiday reveals its intention to be a pilgrimage and goes on being one, day after day. It ended up, more than appropriately, with an invitation to take part in the great High Mass in the abbey on the last Sunday in October, and preach at Evensong, the Feast of Dedication. He knew, he said, it was also *his* feast of dedication and rededication, being, almost to the Sunday, the 25th anniversary of his very first sermon, at Evensong, in the Abbey where he had been ordained at Michaelmas 1963.

Everything was like that on this trip in some odd way. Glastonbury showed a different face to him, and a happier one. There was a kind of "wheel-come-full-circle-but-up-a-few-on-the-spiral" air about everything. Very satisfying, and stimulating too. When he got back home he tore up all his current literary scratchings and suddenly they began to emerge anew – in poetry. There seemed to be a "dynamic" in full flow and he could hardly wait for the next instalment!

On the trip he had come across a copy of my recent book on the Tarot *The Treasurehouse of Images*[10] and enjoyed it immensely. He had always been somewhat nervous of the Tarot, being very conscious at one time about what "gunge" could come up with archetypes if one were not careful. But I had since helped him to see it in a rather different light. Whenever he encountered the Tarot Trumps nowadays he felt a curious affection for them! He had got rid of his old set of Marseilles cards years ago because he felt he did not need it. He had bought it to understand it, and latterly to have compassion for – which he said "is that not the real Name of the Game?"

---

10 Also known as *Tarot & Magic*. Recently issued in expanded edition by Skylight Press, 2012.

The trip had also caused him to notice my *History of White Magic* in his bookcase and fish it out – and found he could not put it down! So he was now having another go at *Experience of the Inner Worlds*. "Must be on a Gareth Knight trip or something!" Somehow it all seemed very relevant, but in a new and different way.

All seemed to be going my way at this time. My *History of White Magic* had led to my being invited to contribute to a television series on *The Gnostics,* and Element Books had come knocking at my door to commission a book, *The Magical World of the Inklings*, developed out of my Hawkwood workshops on C.S.Lewis, J.R.R.Tolkien, Charles Williams and the anthroposophist Owen Barfield.

Element was a new publisher on the scene, and had set up an impressive list with a leaning toward current spirituality – including distribution of Gordon Strachan's book. Fortunately, in their survey of likely talent, Tony Duncan had not gone unnoticed and they commissioned him to write a book of meditations on Christian themes. The result of was *The Mind of Christ*, published in 1990.

In fact the book had already been written, five years before, toward the end of his apparently unproductive Warkworth years. He had sat in a hut at the bottom of his garden, to think things through for himself, and try to write something about God. The only reader was intended to be himself, for as he sat down to write, it was with the words of Meister Eckhart ringing in his ears "Why dost thou prate of God? Whatever thou sayest is untrue!" Which led to him beginning to refer to God as "The Mystery".

This led him to say in his introduction:

There comes a time in every man's life – even a clergyman's life – when a great desire is felt to desist from words altogether and fall silent before THE MYSTERY. It is during the years leading up to this time that one feels compelled to make a noise – to talk, to write – even to teach! Yet, these very activities are perhaps best undertaken when the initial enthusiasms have worn away and there is a certain resistance to the whole thing. A becoming diffidence is appropriate, to be overcome only by a sense of urgency and in a spirit of obedience. I dare to think that something like this compelled the author of this book to put pen to paper.

Every preacher knows the difference between having something to say and having to say something – and so does his congregation! And where books are concerned, particularly religious books, there is a difference between a budding author's great desire to write a book on a certain subject and having one's heart seized by a book which is absolutely determined to be written, even though the author has but the vaguest notions, to begin with, as to what the subject matter might be. For good or ill, this book falls into the second category.

The Mind of Christ was offered as a connected collection of mediations or provocations to meditation – things to think about and mull over in prayer, and although he was a Christian priest he had taken some pains not to be institutionally "churchy".

The Christian Church, he insisted, was in its essence an organism – a living thing – that transcended the boundaries of this life, death and the hereafter. It was however of the nature of organisms to organise, in the process of which they could quickly stifle, or at least obscure, their organisms. But Christ was not to be contained within the four walls of a church building. Nor was he in the back pocket of someone's hierarchy. Our Lord did not come to found a new, better world religion, but to liberate us from religion once and for all!

Jesus Christ, God Incarnate, was too big for religion! There is no Temple in the Heavenly Jerusalem, the Bible tells us that. He hoped that the book would communicate something of the Love of God in which its author abides along with the driving desire to share it with others.

Privately he wrote to me saying that the book wrote itself rather as did *The Lord of the Dance,* but he rather expected that the reviewers of the *Church Times* and their ilk would react to it "like a duck laying a square egg!"

Whatever their reactions may have been, I have to admit that I tended to underestimate it myself at first, not realising it to be a book of private meditations, or provocations to meditation. If one approached it as if reading a sermon it could seem like a collection of dogmatic pronouncements, when what he was really doing was stating a proposition to himself and then following its possible applications through in mystical meditation.

Suffice to say that, I did not squawk like the proverbial duck, but laid it gently aside for some time, before eventually returning to find it to be a guide, philosopher, friend and provoker to meditation leading to a doorway to mystical realisation that I would not be without. I suppose this is what Tony Duncan had earlier meant by the phrase "growing into the measure of the fullness of Christ" some years before, which had not meant much to me at the time. His own great strength of being able to live to the full the life of a much loved parish priest and yet avoid being "churchy" to a wider flock no doubt came to him from his mystical life at the altar, as revealed in the awed sentiments he records in a sonnet from *The Great Work*.

THE CELEBRANT

To stand six feet before the Holy Trinity
with bread and cup: an awesome thing
not to be thought about. Figure of speech,
the words but toys about the Throne of God

left strewn. A Nothing in the Lord's own cloak,
obedient, a focal point am I. No words
are possible yet words are said, the offering left
to lie before the Lord's Life-giving stroke.

And I have seen: the Veil once lifted back
then dropped again. I am but feet upon the ground,
an earth-wire from tremendous things

beyond all saying. I have seen, have seen;
know not, yet understand what here is done:
this Earth made one with Heaven, the Victory won.

Anyhow the book was sufficiently successful for Element to come back to him again for *The Elements of Celtic Christianity*, although he tendered a cautionary note about taking the title of his book too literally.

"It is not about Celtic Christianity at all" he wrote, "because there is no such thing. It is not about the Celtic Church either, because there never was one, separate and definable in such terms. It is about Celtic spirituality, and there is indeed something vitally different and distinct about that." A spirituality notable for its simplicity, austerity and respect for the sanctity of nature, which could come like a breath of fresh air.

The spirituality of the Celt was a calling back to what we are. A recall to reality, to living life with the head in the heart. With a love of the natural world as response to a loving Creator. A vision that had been admirably summed up in the words from the Jesuit poet Gerard Manley Hopkins: *"The world is charged with the grandeur of God."*

And it was not difficult to find similar expression in the verses of Anthony Duncan.

The Month of March

The Blackbirds bicker, chase about;
males chasing males, so neither feeds.
Their wives stand muted, racked with doubt
and tentative. Then urgent needs
prevail and so they peck. Packed tight,
the hands-in-pockets Sparrows strive
with might and main to stay alive,
all cheerful, while their betters fight.

The speckled Starlings, in a crowd,
swarm in to peer, and peck, and strut
two passing Pigeons are allowed,
while Sparrows strive their beaks to shut.
Two heavy Jackdaws in cloth caps
disturb the party, muscle in,
swagger, puff out their chests and grin,
then leave things to the little chaps.

The Tits hang upside-down, attack
the hanging nuts, then come to ground
to scratch and search, fly up and back
and take whatever can be found,
for time is passing, Spring is here.
The cheerful Robin looks about;
no more this winter feed will out
until the dying of the year.

A Cold, Wet April

Fierce rain squalls lash the yard. At every break
a Bluetit flutters to attack the husk
of dangling coconut, urgent to make
a luncheon of it. And the lengthening dusk
is filled with business all along the eaves.
Bright Starlings building all the light-long day
make all about a builder's yard to rob;
and one, beak-laden – long straw, twigs and leaves –
hops thrice, then wings unsteadily away
'till, gutter perched, beaks busy at his job.

The Robin, winter's cheery country squire,
comes seldom; but when nuts hang in their net
the Tits still ravage, hanging on the wire.
The Blackbird and his dowdy wife are yet
half-distant, bickering. She in her place,
his beady, barrack-lawyer's little eye
with bright bad temper glitters. High and fast
across the chilling sky the rain clouds race.
The Rooks are building and their raucous cry
reminds each day of rain that winter's past.

Soup-kitchen time for birds is past and gone.
The crocus blooms above the dry-stone wall;
the feathered market place of woebegone
competitors has but a single stall
remaining, intermittently. And that
most sudden swoop of Seagulls, scattering
the poor, no more. Nor yet shall come again,
respectable, discreet, the Water-Rat
from out the dyke. No more the pattering
of spiky feet, but slanting, lashing rain.

Linhope Spout

Three desperate weeks of driving rain
hurl you, full toss and twisting, down
to crash into your cauldron, strain
and swirl and foam, your flood black-brown,
and thunder, thunder from your walls again.

I know you differently. A spray
of silver sunlight through the green;
a leafy paradise where fairies play
among your gleaming rocks, unseen.
Where mortals linger, may not stay.

A moonlight place are you, where pours
quicksilver down both earth and sky.
A spring and summer world is yours
of cataract and cloud, where high
the bird and high the spirit soars.

But now, Niagara, you tower;
you crash in cataclysmic gloom.
Full elemental in this hour,
too mindful of the crack of doom.
You fascinate with awful power.

High Places

The hilltop shrine, the holy place,
high tension terminal of Heaven and Earth,
of inner and of outer, of the psychic store
of Man in his bewilderment; all quiet now,
fulfilled long since to softer vigils keep
with urgency of bracken, and of heather and the sheep.

The head of stone, the fashioned face,
conceals its countenance and contemplates the Birth
that freed it from the fear, unholy awe –
a cultic slaughterhouse of vice and vow –
yet keeps its memory. Dig not too deep;
tread soft and with compassion. Let it sleep.

Ascension Day in the Garden

A priest, full-fledged from out the apple tree,
drowned deep in *Alleluia*, sings;
invokes, far flung, a rich responsory
from ordinary things.

A hollow hammering on wooden planks
up-village, echoes from stone walls;
the timber, aromatic, offers thanks
through whom its scent recalls.

A diesel engined truck responds the bird
with gearbox and transmission grind;
injection, detonation of the Word,
exhaustive of its kind.

A bird quite other than my feathered friend,
broad-arrow, flashing, with a howl
rips up the sky from end to end
and answers with a growl.

But far and far, and near and near, the song;
a proclamation, made upon
each branch, each tree the river bank along;
"Life *Is!* And Life goes on!"

But there was another important element in Celtic spirituality, that needed consideration: the rediscovery of the feminine principle, and one which he had amply covered, *inter alia*, in *The Mind of Christ*.

That is to say, the acknowledgement by men of their own feminine nature, the complementary release in women of their long suppressed and denied masculine nature, and all the creativity which must accompany it. There was in the whole Celtic tradition a remarkable equilibrium as far as the masculine and the feminine are concerned. Not a complete equilibrium but one remarkably free from the man-dominated, woman-hating (which means woman-fearing) distortions to be found in many other cultures. And which survive, disfiguringly and unfaithfully, in many of the churches of the Christian world.

Much responsibility lay upon the psychology of an early father of the church, St Augustine of Hippo, tormented by guilt centred upon his own sexuality, who identified sex with sin. Tony Duncan had singled him out for poetic comment.

Ode for St. Augustine's Day

You did not know, you good and holy man,
your hang-ups from the pit of hell,
or where free-will and Grace begin
their blessed Baccanal
but churned below, bewildered, turned and ran;
equated sex with sin.

An intellectual, driven from the loins,
you intellectualised embrace,
rejecting it; became a Manichee.
But still you could not face
the abstinence that iron creed enjoins,
preferring ecstasy.

Your mother pestered God with urgent prayers
to prise you from your paramour
and from her child by you, to shove
them from you, slam the door;
dehumanising Woman and her "snares,"
all for the God of Love!

And so you turned, and Apostolic hands
bestowed Episcopal estate.
Right faithfully you served, a prince!
But later, lesser men equate
your hang-ups with God's Truth, bind us in bands.
We've suffered ever since!

And he had similar strictures to address to the hyper intellectual Thomas Aquinas and other fathers of the church who had wrapped the faith in intellectual bands.

Dear Aquinas SV
"To argue for the existence of God is to deny Him" – Karl Barth.

No, dear Aquinas! Put your *Summa* down,
'tis "so much straw!" So faithfully you strove
yet could not see for looking. Look with me
and contemplate the loveliness set down:
Divinity incarnate, interwove
breathtakingly in everything we see.

You call me Pantheist? You silly man!
Throw down your pen, come! Grab a girl and dance
and lose yourself in wonder. Find in her
Divine Compassion. Worship, if you can,
Unutterable Beauty in her glance;
a vision only love's own tears can blur.

Oh yes! I grant you, sin can blur it too;
but come, Aquinas! We are both forgiven
and swim in oceans of forgiveness! Here
is proof enough of God for us to view –
Woman and her Beauty! We are shriven
in our wonderment! Be of good cheer!

And in pursuit of this freeing up of the bands of fear of sex, or the polarity of male and female, we find a theme that runs through much of Tony Duncan's poetry, illuminating many aspects from his own experience, and a "transfiguration" seemingly in agreement with Charles Williams' view of falling in love, that it was not so much an anima or animus projection, as favoured by some psychologists, but a vision of the beloved as seen, created and loved by God. Or even "the Creator through the creature seen!"

Transfiguration

To look is not to see,
for vision is an inward thing
revealing to the inner eye
what it can spy;
what Love is now transfiguring.

It is not you or me
but Love itself that holds us rapt.
Creator through the creature seen,
with all that this can mean.
Thus love, by Love, is gently trapped.

There can none other be.
God is revealed in human guise
when lovers are by Love possessed
and challenged with the Quest
Eternal, seen through loving eyes.

Not that all such visions proceed to a life long commitment. And it seems that Tony Duncan was not short of partners in the preliminary skirmishing of courtship, to judge from this impressive list, stirred by musing through some old photographic negatives.

Forty Years On

Old photographic negatives.
I squint and I puzzle, sort them through
and stir what up from deep unconscious mind?
I threw all these away
decades ago! Now they renew;
invade my *Now* as they were *Then*. Remind:
Loves of another day.

Dear red-haired Millicent, the twin,
who gave up marmalade for Lent
and smote her golf balls with terrific force,
bewitched me for a year.
O with what amorous intent
I heaved her heavy golf-clubs round that course
for very little cheer.

And fair-haired Pam who struck the spark,
dark Sylvia who fanned the flame
and fuelled it by long absence 'till it flared
to flare out at the last.
Dear Theta, evermore the same,
exchanging urgent notes on who had dared
and who, and what, had passed.

And dear, long-legged Barbara!
Long-time first favourite in the stakes
who stirs me still with traces of remorse
for what did not occur.
I was ungenerous, lacked what it takes.
I played but second fiddle to her horse
and lost the race for her.

O Caribbean Norma! Your
most darling womanhood awoke a man
in me I did not know, all armoured for the Quest,
saving maturity.
So naught matured, or went to plan.
You were the loveliest of all, the best:
but it was not to be.

Eternal youth! You stay with me
in timelessness, grandmothers all!
Fulfilled or unfulfilled, blue-rinsed your hair,
one image of you stays.

God's blessing asked in this recall
by one whose joy it was to love, and share
the springtime of your days.

And nor is the magnetic attraction a consequence of adolescence. It goes deeper than this, and in all innocence.

Miah

Where are you now? Where have you gone,
who were to me an opening of my eyes;
a mystery half-revealed, a life begun,
a blessing of surprise?

So has the passing of the years
confirmed my longing heart of love, and awe.
You were to me nor pain, nor tears,
but laughter evermore.

Well I remember, hand in hand,
through lapping wavelets 'neath the bright blue sky,
timeless, nor need to understand,
we'd wander, you and I.

Of love, 'til then, I nothing knew,
but knowing you turned all things into Heaven;
nor yet forgot, nor lost from view.
I was but six and you were seven.

Or in this later experience across the yang and yin divide, perhaps compounded with another powerful archetype of the "miraculous child" – a concatenation of primal innocence and purity of vision.

Nancy's Helen

Down on my Uncle's farm
my heart leapt in alarm;
met archetypal charm
and iron will.
Me, working at the hay
that long gone summer's day
she took my breath away
and holds it still.

The tribal memory stirred;
all space and time were blurred,
for something had occurred
and I was part.
She but a tiny tot,
her flaming hair red hot;
beauty and grace – the lot!
I lost my heart.

She but a tiny child;
myself, both strong and wild –
and neither meek nor mild –
could not approach,
so deep the mystery.
An archetype was she.
I could no closer be
without reproach.

All down the years since then,
mired in the world of men,
I fain would know again
what I knew there.
My pitchfork in the hay,
a blazing summer's day –
bewitched, and lost for aye
in flaming hair!

And much of his poetry concerning the dynamics of love is expressed in middle age, with the ability to look back on past raging desires for possession in an appreciation of beauty for its own sake.

Love, Youth and Age

Am I in love with Love, perhaps,
who, lingering, look on lissom grace,
adoring every pretty face
yet unconcerned to run that race,
competing with those younger chaps?

They – bondsmen still – they need to own;
exclusively to have and hold;
all insecure, however bold.
They do not know, cannot be told
the Mystery of Love, and Love alone.

Worn out are they, by passions flung.
Come, lads! Stand back; see and adore,
then fall in wonder to the floor
as I have done, now gone before
who, being old, am ever young.

And there follow a few examples of this maturer vision and appreciation of love and beauty, whether it be a young girl dawning into womanhood –

Melissa

I, who am older now, do see
her full-fledged into beauty born.
Translucent and a frailty
to touch the heart in this, her dawn
of womanhood. No child of mind
but child of light, of fairyland.
While all come crowding for her hand,
my manhood muses at her shrine.

I, who am older now, well know
those joys, those sorrows yet to feel;
and that her heart and hands must show,
through woman's weakness, strength of steel;
for she is Woman. Yet to be:
the mystery of her self, fulfilled.
But that it shall be, and is willed,
I, who am ever young, can see.

Or in the more casual context of everyday life, a stranger in a supermarket:

The Girl at the Check-Out

I could not tell her she was beautiful;
she'd be embarrassed, quite misunderstand.
So young, so callow and so dutiful
at all the duties cash-desks can demand.
She smiled and put the change into my hand;
our eyes met briefly and her cheeks were flushed.
I smiled and left, my place to understand.
Grandfatherly am I, no hopes were crushed
as were I fifty years the younger. Hushed
those hurts, objective now and dutiful,
I worship thankfully, no longer rushed.
I could not tell her she was beautiful,
Our God is Love, all beauty we adore
and she, a woman, woman's beauty wore.

And also in the exercise of his ministry, conscious of the limitations of social convention.

Love Lies Bleeding

Shall you so live, a water-fly;
on surface tension so rely;
too frightened yet to swim or fly,
lacking all strength?
And must you keep, lest all shall die,
love at arm's length?

Shall you, so sinned against, so sin?
So fearful yet to look within
Lest, sudden stirred, there shall begin
something not known?
Must all be black? Must all cave in;
be overthrown?

Would to dear God what's in my heart
my arms might teach! Might play some part
in bringing you to better start
and see you through
to love, from love no more apart;
for love of you.

Or in this celebration of a family visit to Gran Canaria where it appears he was a great hit socially, and even had some of his poems translated and published in Spanish.

Spanish Girls

Thanks be to God for Spanish girls!
And thanks to God for eyes to see,
for heart's compassion and delight;
for all that they have meant to me.

Young queens of heaven and dancers all,
they move with straight and tender grace;
an awesome loveliness abides
behind each stern but gentle face.

All angels in an earthly heaven,
yet women all; and in them lies
that Mystery of Love that shines
from out those all-revealing eyes.

But when all is said and done, there were the deeper realisations, as expressed and lived out in his life with Helga, of what lifelong love is all about.

Holy Matrimony

Transfigured each in others' eyes,
so is it now, so was it then;
Eternal Lover each in other knowing.
Forever taken by surprise
to turn again and yet again,
on each the Everlasting Love bestowing.

Our love an icon of the Real,
indwelt, in Love abiding;
its mysteries The Mystery revealing.
Yet many wounds there are to heal,
our frailties colliding;
failures forgiven all, no more concealing.

The Mystery reveals; and we,
though we remain unseeing,
icons of Grace-in-Nature's undertaking
our privilege to be;
in sacramental being,
Creator with creation's marriage-making.

Not that there is not a less elevated side to all of this, but one equally profound in the expression of a commitment between the sexes.

A Husband's View of a Pedestrian Precinct

No place for men is this! The crowd
from hither zigzags off to thither;
canned music snatches, brash and loud,
and women purposefully dither,
intent on purchase. Men in hats,
bewildered, lost and ill at ease,
their wives bag-laden, refugees,
return to cars parked free on rubble and brickbats.

A horrid place is this! But good
for shopping, car and lorry free.
Shoppers' Elysium, and understood
by housewives, yet no place for me
awaiting wife's return, replete.
I loiter while my spirit drops;
young mothers scowl about the shops
and jab their angry push-chairs at my feet.

Or even this more intimate encounter on a shopping expedition:

OBSERVATIONS OF A GENTLEMAN FRIEND

Her Paradise is in a rail of clothes.
like moth in candle-flame, her cheque-book burns
as down she falls, discarding these and those,
revealing lace and lingerie, She turns:

ecstatic indecision. This? Or that?
She smooths and preens, and looks into a glass,
and twists; regards her bottom. Will it pass?
Then, glowing, makes an entrance through the veil,
all lovely in this Look that shall prevail.

Dear Lady, you are purring like a cat!

But when all is said and done, most moving is perhaps this poem about the moving on of a deep relationship, when family are grown and flown.

TRAVELLING LIGHT

We have each other. All the rest is gone
yet lingers, loved, familiar, while we stay;
old friends and faithful, soon to be passed on;
ourselves in transit, soon to be away.
So very few things matter now, but we
who have each other are secure and fast,
for things possessed have turned to persons known;
possessions and ourselves are both set free
and all are passing and will soon be past.
And though we linger to the very last
there is no loss; we shall not be alone.

We have each other, and when all is said
and done there is no more, our needs are met.
And come that day when one of us is dead,
gone on ahead, the other lingering yet,
we have each other and may rest secure.
And when particularity is past
and Love embracing everything is known,
and all things have each other and endure
in that abiding Joy, secure and fast,
in which our special joy shall ever last;
we have all things, who never were alone.

At which point of mutual compassion it is perhaps appropriate to recall that the major part of his duties at Whitley Mill was as Hexham hospital chaplain, a line of ministry which he welcomed and had done before as a hospital visitor, despite the testing emotional challenges, some of which he recorded here.

The Hospital Chaplain

The temptation: to affect an easy expertise,
compete in aura of white coats and stethoscopes
and play their game. I am too painfully aware
of wandering the wards with empty hands,
but this my calling: to be wide open, free,
and trust that God's own Grace will work in me.

The day begins and ends in great unease,
with muted expectations and uncertain hopes.
I am a priest whose task is to be there;
a heart perambulating, reconciling hands,
a vehicle of compassion. The profoundest Grace?
To be a piece of furniture about the place!

THE DAY ROOM

The day room has its trigger of despair.
A trip-wire lurks among the walking frames
and threads, invisible, among these chairs
all facing inwards, occupied in vacancy
by inward facing, nearly vacant lots.

My conversations stretch and strain,
search wildly for a touch-down. While
the big screen flickers meaningless
to all the inturned faces, all awash
in crackling babble, mega-volumed sound.

I tread, tip-toed among the tripwires,
and wonder why I come, yet know
I must. I dodge between the walking frames
and smile, and say a word or two – and start:
a bolt of blackness thuds into my heart.

THE SPINAL WARD

My senses, my imagination numb,
I move between the tilting beds;
pass time of day and chatter,
and move on. And shortly go away
upon two legs – the cruellest part.

For it is all too much and I am dumb.
No words will serve. Heroic shreds
of broken lives, the trivia that matter
to despair; I can for these but kneel and pray
in Christ's compassion and in His broken heart.

And likewise in visiting the sick in their homes:

Peace

She will die quite soon
and tidies up her memories.
Her past and present gathered up,
presented with compassion. So
pass the days in this old house;
her peace transfiguring.

Elizabeth

Her bedsit life is done.
She lies now in a canvas bag;
two flights of stairs await.

The neighbour's key is in the lock,
the landing doors stand half ajar;
behind them, neighbours wait.

The van door closes. Now no more
that tragic face will pass my door.
All over now, her fate.

At times facing up to a sense of inadequacy, or inability to rise to expectations of the desperate in a ministry of healing.

The Healer

I laid on hands and prayed;
the man was dead before the sun
came round to where it stood
to shine upon my ministry,
old people, blessed to die,
pass on and I pass by
to pray again, come Wednesday.

I laid on hands and prayed,
and darkness fled; too dark
for my unknowing. A remit,
a chance not taken, death
returned, the chance was lost.
He died, and I am conscience-tossed;
yet back to work, come Wednesday.

I laid on hands and prayed.
The darkness writhed and shrivelled up,
all spitted on the angel's sword.
I know not what is wrought in me;
God's mysteries, I have no part
save laying bare to death my heart
to die again, come Wednesday.

Or these savage lines about assumed mental illness.

THE PROPHET

God spoke to him.
His world looked oddly at him,
turned away. Outcast
upon the very fringe of life
he wandered past their half-turned backs
and went on living, lone.

He lost his job.
They sent for him, examined him
and sought their ease by drugging him
and jolting from his tortured brain
all thoughts of it:
lest God should speak to him again.

The time was coming, however, for another challenge, that of retirement. Having come to the ministry at a comparatively advanced age, he fell into the Pensions Board "penniless" category. Where to try to settle? So far, Brampton in Cumbria seemed a likely spot. But in the course of a career of thirty-five years, "moving on" was a condition to which he had become to some extent reconciled.

The Wild Goose Flighted

I have not lingered long enough
to root into the ground;
nor ever lived in my own land
but moved round and around
from counties South to counties North,
and sailed across the sea.
From house to house, as I go forth,
my home abides in me.

Nor never I a freeholder
nor owned a plot of land;
my clan's own myth my history
for thus I understand.
Through all the world, with each foot's fall,
I find my place and part;
embrace it all and carry all
its songs within my heart.

And there was always a great emotional wrench in leaving a parish behind, let alone a life's work.

The Parish Priest Retired

To let all go is life indeed,
a dying but to live.
That "cure of souls both mine and thine",
the final thing to give.

Last Sunday; party in the hall,
and I am history.
My "then" is past, for all is "now",
such is *The Mystery*.

Vacate the stall and walk away,
and never once look back.
Leave all the loves at Love's command;
heart broken on the rack.

Leave all who love, that I have loved,
and suffered long and deep
for Love's own sake. Not mine to take;
some other shepherd's sheep.

My joy: to hear odd scraps of news;
who lives, and who has died;
recall – and then let go again.
In God we all abide.

For letting go is life indeed;
time to *become*, and *be*.
Fulfilment of what was, and is
all in *The Mystery*.

And remembering some of those he left behind in these amusing lines full of love, expressed in the local dialect, for which he had a natural gift, whether it be rural Gloucestershire or Northumbria.

Prospect of a Garden Party

It might could come oot agin, likely,
wi' a nice bit o' wind there, foreby,
ta dry up the ground a bit. Canny!
'Tis the best! Forst weekend o' July!

We'll best get the tables fra' Chapel.
Mind! Liza'll play war viv us yet
if the boiler's still leakin fra' last year!
Hope it divn't justs come away wet!

Whitley Mill

The lads wiv a tractor and trailor
will howk the chairs doon fra' the Haall;
but we'll not can forget the bit cover
ower Elsie's White Elephant Staall!

The Bottle Staall's got the tarpaulin,
the Lemonade's needin' a chair;
there's a canny bit forcast in Telly,
but it might could just come away there!

There is posters all ower the Village;
an advortisment in the Gazette.
We'll mak mebby var nigh a thousand –
if it divn't just come away wet!

Tony with his son, son-in-law and grand-daughter at Whitley Mill, 1988

8

CORBRIDGE

Despite some worries over what life after retirement might be on the pittance of a parson's pension, Tony and Helga Duncan found a congenial resting place at Corbridge, a village some 4 miles east of Hexham. It was to be the closest that Tony came to living in his beloved Scotland, but not too far off as Corbridge (then known as Corstopitum) had once been the most northerly town in the Roman Empire and served as a supply base for the troops on Hadrian's Wall. In the middle ages it had been second only to Newcastle in size and prosperity in the north east. It also turned out to be the place where Tony Duncan began to enjoy unprecedented success with his writing. It was as if some kind of genie had come out of the bottle coincident with his retirement. The first indications of which were some very unlikely items that arrived on my door mat toward the end of 1995.

The first of these came with a note:

> Here is the booklet I wrote for my successors as "spooks" ministry men. It has the distinction of having passed muster with the Chairman of the Church of England Doctrine Commission. Can one fly higher?
> I hope it will be of some use.

Entitled *The Psychic Disturbance of Places* it was a 23-page document detailing quite a lot of the stuff that he had been up to, along with Dom Robert Petitpierre, back at Parkend, and which he had always refused to discuss in any detail.

The guide, restricted to ministers of the Church of England, consisted of notes concerning the diagnosis of causes of psychically disturbed places and suggested ministries for their clearance based on twenty-five years experience in this field. It did not deal with problems of disturbed or "possessed" persons, with which the author felt he did not have sufficient experience. Thus the phenomena he dealt with came under the headings of (1) Place Memories, (2) Poltergeist phenomena, (3) Ghosts proper, and (4) the Demonic.[11]

Experience suggested that *Place Memories* were a mechanism of sorts wherein certain past events left behind visual or auditory phenomena that were somehow etched into the place of their occurrence – rather like a psychic video or audio recording. Two sets of circumstance seemed most likely to "record" themselves – a scene of high and usually distressed emotion, or an action regularly repeated over a considerable period of time.

One example of an auditory place memory was a once-a-year sound of luggage being hurled down a staircase, when a former occupant had been thrown out by his father after a catastrophic family row. Another was the sound of the smashing of a huge staircase window where a baby had been thrown through following some cataclysmic family upset. In both cases though, not everyone heard the sounds; some were completely unaware of them.

An example of a visual place memory of a regularly repeated action was that of a Victorian housemaid carrying a bundle of linen across a room and disappearing through the wall. She was only visible, however, above the knees, on account of the floor having been raised some eighteen inches since her day, her image walking on the old floor and passing through a partition wall that had once not been there. Another example involved a lady witnessing a scenario including small children in Victorian dress, who turned out to be her own mother, uncles and aunts, now middle aged, not only still alive but also currently present in the house. Plainly not ghosts, although the Victorian maid in the previous example could possibly have been!

A feature of all such "recordings" was that they only appeared to someone who was psychically sensitive to the appropriate degree, with the witness providing an unconscious source of energy – which could leave them feeling somewhat "drained" or with a feeling of chill in the air. On the whole, however, such experiences were more puzzling than alarming, and seldom an occasion for calling in the vicar!

The word *Poltergeist*, which simply means a "noisy ghost" covered a broad range of phenomena. The classic type of poltergeist was often associated with the presence of a child, usually a boy, at the onset of

---

11 Indeed the Bishop of Exeter's Commission on Exorcism regarded the concept of personal demonic possession to be extremely dubious, and that any alleged case should be referred to a specialist in psychological medicine for assessment as to mental or physical illness.

puberty. The child has no control over the phenomena, and whilst never threatened by them, is as puzzled and disturbed as everybody else. Phenomena can include the moving of objects, noises, raps, bumps in the night (or daytime), scratching, occasionally a voice mumbling or calling a name. In one quite spectacular case a young boy had only to carry a glass or cup of liquid across a room – tea, coffee, cola, water etc – for the same liquid to begin dripping from the ceiling above him, though without leaving any mark. The suggestion was made "Try him with whisky!" but the disturbance was quieted by the laying on of hands with prayer. This, together with a blessing of the house for good measure, was thus really a Ministry of Healing rather than Deliverance.

A *Ghost* generally turned out to be human being who for one reason or another was "earthbound" in a post-mortem state, usually with a suggestion of something left unfulfilled. A number of causes for their condition included ignorance of the fact of their own death – not so bizarre as it sounds – having died suddenly and finding themselves conscious and still in very closely earth related circumstances, to continue in a kind of confused dream world until reality breaks in and they can pass on.

More deliberate could be obsession with home or workplace or with a still-living person. One old cook was so obsessed with her kitchen that she caused the resignation of a succession of living cooks by the perpetual atmosphere of disapproval, removing trays from tables and causing rugs to drag themselves across the floor. Obsession with a still living person was almost always morbid, as in the case of another former domestic who was devoted to the teenage "young master" of the house, or a great-grandfather so besotted with his great-granddaughter that he began to haunt the new bungalow where she lived quite shortly after having been buried in the churchyard.

Perhaps most tragic were cases of fear of having committed an unforgivable sin (not uncommonly to do with some terrible deed in war) an example being a very sad man who haunted a house just outside Tewkesbury for many years, standing by an upstairs window gazing across the common. Eventually, having been able to contact him after a long time in prayer, reciting the General Confession with him and pronouncing formal absolution, he felt able to move on, the house was no longer haunted and a great peace pervaded it. It was of first importance to remember that in most of these cases, one was dealing with a fellow human being in need of help. Normal priestly compassion, gentleness – and occasionally firmness – being called for in a normal priestly way, of absolution rather than banishment.

A separate chapter was devoted to consideration of the *Demonic*, or encounters with objective evil. For most purposes it might be regarded as axiomatic that the demonic was only encountered where grave human sin had offered it an entry, whereafter it fed and grew more potent depending on what opportunities were given to it. Occasions of such would include (a) a serious crime, such as murder, (b) a life given over to hatred, resentment or cruelty, (c) a life dedicated to the domination and manipulation of others, (d) gross betrayals of trust, particularly toward the young, (e) sites formerly used for human sacrifice, (f) places (including some church buildings) in which Satanic or other Black Magical rituals have taken place, (g) places in which psychic activities have taken place, of an irresponsible or self-deluding character, (h) the business premises of organisations dedicated, less to legitimate commerce, than to greed, ruthlessness and the acquisition of power.

It was best in these cases to avoid any speculation about Satan or of the Devil but to follow Dom Robert Petitpierre's practice of regarding them simply as "little devils" in his book *Exorcising Devils* (Robert Hale, 1976). And Anthony Duncan recommended to his clerical brethren, for practical purposes, the SPCK book *Exorcism,* edited by Dom Robert Petitpierre, the findings of a Commission convened by the Bishop of Exeter following some unhealthy and near-hysterical publicity given to the subject in 1963. It recommended that every diocesan bishop should appoint a diocesan exorcist to assist the local vicar, who was the first port of call in any such problem.

I realised that some of Tony Duncan's poems had referred to events such as these, arising from personal experience.

THE ANNIVERSARY

The sorry groan of grief long since,
half-heard by the unheeding, falls
in mumblings from containing walls
which play again old memories
to those whose wavebands match their own.

A shade of midnight rattles soft,
yet loud enough to waken, on
a half-remembering bedroom door
and dithers, shy in shadows;
remembering a long-since death.

Both play their tapes upon a heart
and mind which fits their reel;
but what will they awaken:
Fear, or Prayer?

The Rectory

They would wake to hear a new-born baby cry,
sit up in bed alarmed, put on the light,
then dressing-gowned, get up and walk about;
pause briefly by the empty attic stair,
conclude they had been dreaming and forget their fright.

She read her book then, sleepy, settled down,
reached for the switch. She'd heard that sound before!
The house was locked and empty but for her
and two small dogs. Look out she did not dare
but pushed the chest of drawers across the door.

The sad old house was crumbling and decayed;
steep roofed and gothic, built in better days
and hung with memories. A rector and his maid –
girl from the village likely – now released by prayer
are reconciled, have gone their separate ways.

Portrait of a Predecessor

Your anxious countenance disturbs my peace.
We are acquainted in another age,
a dispensation long since past
but still transcending. Here you died
worn out and disillusioned. Now
you follow me with anxious eyes
half-knowing, but in ignorance
of what defeated you. My friend,
stand back a little; hold me in your prayer
that such another come not to your end.

He had, in the meantime, struck a chord with his books on Celtic spirituality, for HarperCollins, a major international publishing house who had subsequently gobbled up Aquarian Press, commissioned him to compile *A Little Book of Celtic Prayer* for their Marshall Pickering imprint. This was something of an irony insofar that he had felt turning out a book of prayers distinctly unattractive back at Warkworth. However, the fact that it was to be a compendium of Celtic prayers put a light of a different colour upon the prospect, and his Introduction was particularly valuable guidance on the character of Celtic Spirituality and the importance of "heart and hearth centred" religion.

> Perhaps the greatest single calamity to overtake Western Christianity in recent centuries has been the divorce of the head from the heart and the exaltation of the former over the latter. In large part, this is a product of the Renaissance, translated into religious terms by the cataclysmic upheavals of the Reformation.
>
> During this period, in reaction against superstition – real and supposed – reason was exalted and intuition was discounted, even feared and denied. In this climate, religion became to a very large degree head-centred rather than heart-centred, and Sunday religion began, slowly and inexorably, to part company with the religion of the hearth. We, in our generation, are the inheritors of the fruits of this troubled period.
>
> Celtic spirituality, as we are now discovering it, is the religion of the hearth. It is also the religion of what, in terms more familiar to our Orthodox brethren, we might described as "the mind in the heart".

> There is no flight from reason in Celtic spirituality; very far from it. Nor is there any flight from intuition either. The Celt is above all a realist. Poet he may be – he may choose to define himself more naturally in terms of myth than in those of history, a profoundly valid thing to do – but there is none of the "Celtic Twilight" about the Celt! His feet are on the ground, and very firmly set.
>
> Celtic spirituality is deeply Trinitarian. In addition, it presupposes a wholeness within which there is no possibility of separation between the farmer, his cow, the saints in heaven, the holy angels, the mother of God and the ever-loving Triune Creator.
>
> The beauty of nature is always a reflection – even an icon – of its Creator. There is no conceivable distinction made between "religion" and "life". Life is lived in the unselfconscious and utterly natural relationship of beloved creature and beloved Creator, and in company with all other beloved creatures in Heaven and upon Earth.

This was much the same message as he had been trying to put across in *The Priesthood of Man* that had caused such raised eyebrows in the *Church Times* back in 1973. Only now he was able to address a less intellectually hidebound and conservative readership.

And on the poetry front he seemed to have broken through to a new level in a sequence of seven poems, called *The Spheres,* which he sent along to me with a laconic note:

> Following on from the *Lord of the Dance* and the excitements of the last few weeks, I thought you might be interested in the enclosed which seems to indicate "where I am at" – so to speak. Perhaps I am "nuts" – but it is not a disagreeable state, so be reassured.

They are not an easy read but merit considerable study – with the heart as well as the head.

The Sphere of Silence

I passed through the centre of my sphere of silence;
passed through my heart into my inmost heart
which opened to Infinity. And there was shown to me
a myriad of shining spheres. The Dance is danced,
yet all at the centre of my inmost heart

which was, and is, Infinity. The hand
which, taking my hand, brought me Everywhere,
made gesture. I know not, then or now, but understand.

I am to be a door between the dancing spheres.
All paths upon the Tree converge in me;
between my portals all the pilgrims pass
from sphere to sphere, to spheres within
and ever inner, ever wider, ever more and more.
My part – to BE. To be the open door.

My portals rooted, I am Everywhere
and share the Lordship of this Cosmic Dance,
Christ's Fool by invitation. Set in stone,
I tread my measure, dancing on the spot
that all may dance through me, such is my part;
my mind wide open in an open heart.

The context of all this? A love-affair!
The quest for meaning of my self and soul,
Led on in Love; for Meaning and my inmost Self
would Lovers be and in their flight,
the dancing of their measure, in their sweet desire,
I am at one, made whole, and kept entire.

The Castle of the Heart

Transfixed by light, I enter the Great Hall
and find them waiting. Here am I,
a multitude of persons, each to embrace,
acknowledge and accept – each one to integrate
in heart and mind, each one a part of me –
that we become what I am called to be.

Transfixed by light, I enter the Great Hall
and find them waiting. Here are they
who walk beside me on the Earthly planes,
and they on planes transcending, from Beyond,
who answer, silently, my silent prayer,
prayed far beyond them but reflected there.

That Great Hall in the castle of my heart
leads on to mystery. A doorway stands,
half-hid and farthest corner set, and low,
such as requires a stoop to enter. A veil
is parted. Within is neither sound nor sight
but stillness; adoration of the Uncreated Light.

That Great Hall in the castle of my heart
has outer baileys, courts and walls.
A great gate stands, its drawbridge down;
looks out on spreading forests, fields
and God's great challenge: other men.

I must ride hence to live my days
and may not cease, nor gain my Quest,
nor come upon Christ's Holy Grail
until I find it in another's heart,
and all are welcome to my Hall as guest.

Finding and Losing

From out the Great Hall of my inmost heart
a narrow doorway beckons. Beyond, a stair
both winding up and winding down,
unlit. Here must I come with friends
so far; thereafter, go alone,
ascending or descending as my heart is shown.

The labyrinthine workings and the darkest depths
demand my delving from the downward stair.
Beneath lie prisoners, long-lost and fettered, foul;
each one a person of my total man
to be released, acknowledged face to face,
brought up into the Light to take his place.

The stair winds upwards into total loss;
such is my Quest. Imagination stilled,
no hand-holds for the scrambling mind,
nor metaphor, nor myth, their symbols fled;
all gathered for the giving, neither sight nor sound;
consigned to total loss but, in the losing, found.

The Child of Earth

I am of Earth, experience her mysteries,
encounter planes of being not my own;
am touched by worlds on wavelengths other.

In timelessness their times converge;
I know them, though I know them not,
but in my timeless, inmost heart,
and keeping to my own appointed spot
most finely balanced, recognize my part
as one aloof, detached, compassionate – and brother.

The inner spheres, so do they seem,
impinge upon me, touch my heart and mind.
Compassion must accept and take, detached,
the understandings given, may not seek to know
lest knowledge a manipulation seek, nor see
what's hid, but let Creation be.

The shadowlands between those inner spheres,
the dream-worlds that the un-dead dream,
past time in Timelessness encapsulate,
the nightmares, self-invoked, and all their fears:
these Christ, and Christ alone, may penetrate.

I am of Earth, partaker of her mysteries
which, in a figure, I have seen.
The outer spheres of Earth embrace, extend,
are lost in mystery; worlds without end.

THE CHILD OF HEAVEN

Inhabitants of other spheres than this
draw near the threshold of my conscious mind.
As they are sent, perhaps? Or I am bidden?
Some come to see the priest. Others collide,
and we regard in mutual puzzlement
and gently move our worlds once more apart.
I must be vigilant. Four-square must I abide;
discernment and compassion in my heart.

The spheres of Earth have each their outer form
on wavelengths myriad, both close and far,
which give expression to reality within;
each one a facet, each in its place,
unique and interwoven. The totality:
the outward face of Earth's own mystery.

The outer and the inner spheres of Earth
experience the Universe from where each stands,
each with co-ordinates of time and space;
the outer life of each unseeing and opaque.
Yet each one with a teeming life within,
and archetypal of its outward face.
Within, all lives of common life partake,
transcending spheres; the Earth turned outside-in.

I am of Heaven and experience her Mysteries.
My manhood taken up from Earth which is my home,
I am one person of a myriad, for I am Man.
With Man incarnate in my flesh and blood
I am of Heaven, transcending all Earth's spheres.
But where I stand, of this dear Earth a part,
wherever in Eternity mankind is found,
I hold it in compassion in my Heavenly heart.

Love's Journeyings

Things are quite other than they, outward, seem.
So too the skies both of outer and of inner night,
as they are seen from wavelengths other, so they change
and other worlds are entered, other lives are lived;
yet all life back to Life, the source of life is flown.
Life lives all life and is by all lives known.

So may the human soul, by Grace, extend
with arms outstretched, but yet blindfold her eyes
lest knowledge blind her, lead her heart astray;
lest she is never to the Holy Wisdom come
but, maddened by Reality, dismiss it as a dream.
Things are quite other than they, outward, seem.

Love's journeyings between the myriad worlds
are made in quest of an integrity
which is beginningless and has no end;
the very worlds created for this very quest
and modified eternally. Such is the plan;
the context in The Mystery for creature, Man.

Love's journeyings between the myriad worlds
depend upon a wholeness of integrity
beginningless, begotten, without end,
through whom all worlds were made for this great quest.
The quest itself is modified; a change of plan
to rescue, raise and deify the creature, Man.

He who shall wing through inner space
wings independent of the outward form
and is of Love and on love's errands flown.
all else is counterfeit. Thus men by rockets raised
adventure to frustration. Yet their trails of fire
express, though all unconscious, Man's own heart's desire.

All Things Converge

As Universe and Universe converge, the heavens fall
into their melting-pots. Reordering of Inner Space
is consequent upon a change of Mind; a train of thought
pursued towards a new fulfilment. Hands are stretched
across infinities of inner depths to seek, to find
a hand beyond imagining by either questing mind.

Both Outer Space and Outer Spaces are a void
through which all meaning falls to nothingness,
yet are reflections of the Inner; the Abyss of Love
from which all lives, and loves, and beings well
to everlasting overflow. Whose tidal surge
shall rock the heavens as Universe and Universe converge.

The heavens fall into their melting-pots,
Great Heaven transcending. So Universe and Universe
converge, Great Heaven transcending to embrace
an Inner Space made new, the old fulfilled.
New Heaven and New Universe are brought to birth
and, new, with all its gleaming spheres, the Earth.

Great Heaven contains the heavens of Earth
and is their melting-pot. Thus they converge;
are set to mingle and refine, melt down
into Reality with all made new.
Angels and Archangels, to a common plan,
prepare the Advent of the Son of Man.

Even if I could not fully understand them at the time, I was impressed by the deep resonances they expressed. In one sense they constituted a summing up and moving on from the sequence of rubrics from *The Lord of the Dance* and *The Sword in the Sun* on which my book *Experience of the Inner Worlds* was based and that I had used to train the members of the Gareth Knight group. The last stage of which was to come upon a stairway going up and down, not simply in occult meditation but in mystical contemplation. Here, I now realised, were the "Spheres of *Inner Space*" through which the soul could come to realisation of its origins and purpose. In effect, a transformation and transcendence of the conception of the "Spheres of the *Inner Planes*" as generally understood by students of the Qabalistic Tree of Life. It had also been hinted at in the following two poems:

How Many Heavens?

How many heavens does this Earth contain?
What subtleties of wavelength and what bounds
are set? What frequencies are tuned,
what lives are lived upon another plane?

For I have felt them passing by,
intent upon their business, and have seen,
have glimpsed their presence, known them near,
befriended in the corner of an eye.

All life is one. We rise or fall
each persons of one creature: Man.
Our mystery proceeds to plan;
one Inner Space contains us all.

Becoming

I fumbled to become myself,
imprisoned in a consciousness
which played upon illusions.
I sought to circumscribe the All,
embrace the Absolute – but now
I fall into the waiting arms
of darkness, and am shown the light;
I look for nothing, and am given sight.

Technically speaking, the "one Inner Space that contains us all" is another way of expressing the Ain Soph Aur – or Limitless Light that surrounds and infuses the Tree as well as being behind its creation.

However, apart from these deep and lofty concerns, the poems of *The Spheres* contained some unexpected and rather startling down to earth dynamics, as a follow up letter expressed.

The dynamics that occasioned part at least of the poems I sent you (probably the last two or three) manifested again this morning as I found my attempts to read Mattins punctuated with light-hearted jingle. What followed I enclose herewith. It pretty exactly describes some of the less expected goings-on either side of my retirement. Helga and I have often ended up giggling at the absurdity of reality – so to speak. I am always encouraged by the funny side of things. When things don't seem to have a funny side I get very suspicious…There is even a funny side to having pins stuck in one. Read on!

This was accompanied with a trio of what he called "light hearted jingles" which I assumed at the time to be a rather laboured and overblown joke.

The A.U. XI

It started in the usual way;
No Spectre, Spook or shout,
But simply that insistent sense
That 'someone' was about.

I found them by the kitchen sink,
All lined up, tall and grave,
And apprehensive, ill at ease,
All 'trying to be brave!'

'It's OK,' said my Angel chum,
'They're Kosher – more or less!
'Just say "The Lord be with you,"
'Smile and, while you're at it, bless.'

The tension left the atmosphere,
The ice, it seemed to break
And I felt free to try to grasp
The point they sought to make.

'Our Universes,' so I sensed.
'Within their common Source,
'Are gently and most kindly set
'Upon Collision Course.'

CORBRIDGE

They loomed there, by the kitchen sink,
Deliberate and slow,
'We thought we'd cross the Inner Space
'And come and say "hallo!"'

They came and went for weeks on end
And clearly felt at ease;
They set up shop around the fridge
And sat on the deep-freeze.

Clairvoyant Iain spotted them
And guessed they came from far.
Then one of them drove home with him
In the aura of his car.

Perhaps the 'turbo' turned him on?
Inscrutable, their ends.
They gently checked each other out
And parted, best of friends.

They followed with our furniture
And helped us to unpack
Then, slow and grave as ever, said:
'Bye-bye now! We'll be back!'

Oh! Send for the Psychiatrist!
Is madness, this, or sin?
Oh! Send for the Psychiatrist!
And give him a stiff gin!

The E.T. 1st XI

'They're E.T.,' said my Angel chum,
'There's no need for alarm.
'Be nice, and make them feel at home,
'They won't do any harm.'

They knocked politely at the door
And waited in the hall.
I turned the telly off, and prayed,
Then went and found them all.

There was an awkwardness at first
But blessings make amends;
With 'something Cosmic' going on
They'd just come to make friends.

They knocked upon the door again
Much later in the night.
'Was it all right for them to leave?'
Good manners! And polite!

They came again and tapped the door
And waited in the hall.
'I'd really meant it when I'd said
"How nice to see them all?"'

They sent their contact-chap who said
'Their present job was done
'But they'd be back, he'd keep in touch
'And wasn't it such fun?'

Do phone for the Psychiatrist.
Be careful what you tell.
Do phone for the Psychiatrist.
He might not feel quite well!

The E.T. 2nd XI

There is another breed of these,
Somewhat inclined to prank.
Triangular of countenance
And spindly of shank.

By technologic wavelength-shift
They visit pastures new.
We find ourselves the subjects of
Surveillance and review!

They rather freely wander out
And freely wander in;
Regard the likes of you and me
As sorts of 'specimin!'

And thus it was, at dead of night,
Although he meant no harm,
One little blighter, bold as brass,
Stuck needles in my arm!

'They've tagged you!' said my Angel chum,
'It's awfully infra-dig!
'You do as much – and worse – you know
'To polar-bear, or pig!'

The First Eleven sent their chap,
Regretful and polite;
Assured me that it wasn't them!
He hoped I was alright!

Don't send for the Psychiatrist.
Don't let him near, I pray!
Don't send for the Psychiatrist.
He'll lock himself away.

I did not realise that all this doggerel should be taken more seriously until some years later when, sorting through his papers, I came upon a sober account of all this, in prose, which openly and frankly examined the experience of psychic awareness of "extra-terrestrial" contacts, and the theological consequences that this implies; entitled *To Think Without Fear* along with a related paper *The Liberation of the Imagination* and which I earmarked for publication by Skylight Press.[12]

---

12 Scheduled for publication 2014.

I had however, a couple of unexpected works of my own to send his way. One was entitled *The Abbey Papers* and the other *An Introduction to Ritual Magic,* each of which had, in its way, a connection with my esoteric mentor, the late Dion Fortune. The first had come about after I was asked by the Society of the Inner Light to select and edit a volume of her war letters.[13] This had an unexpected consequence. I found myself being contacted by three of her inner plane teachers with whom she had worked since 1922. For ninety days I was asked to sit quietly and write down the words and ideas that were dropped into my head. The resulting script, received at about three times my usual speed of writing, described an elaborate and multi-faceted image of an "Inner Abbey" to serve as a focal point for a wide variety of meditational purposes. I was not quite sure how Tony Duncan might react to them on account of one of the communicators – rather like one of C.G.Jung's contacts – had a track record of being more of a Neoplatonist than a Christian. However, the other two were Christian enough, and the pattern of the abbey was quite similar to Tewkesbury abbey, with one or two purpose built additions.

I need not have worried. Tony Duncan wrote back to say:

Thank you indeed for the copy of the chat-up from the three wise men – three canny lads as we would say in these parts. It is some read! And self authenticating in a very decided fashion indeed.

I am familiar with the Abbey in question, and on a number of levels too. It was nice to see yet another series of "angles" which were new but entirely familiar in that very agreeable way that the right things have. A quite splendid presentation, all in all, and very distinct and agreeable characters doing the presenting. And what a lot of mind clearing stuff in it! I found myself nodding with approval almost as if I was a Yogi clearing a stiff neck!

"This needs a wider audience!" I found myself saying. Yes, but easier said than done. I hope it doesn't have to wait twenty years like some stuff I could tell of! But that only goes to show that things have their own time and the unexpected happens when its time comes round.

I was particularly pleased to see the Tarot redeemed. Twenty years ago it was rather dismissed by my informant – though not without the acknowledgement that it was capable of being cleansed of its cobwebs and

---

13 *Dion Fortune's Magical Battle of Britain*, Golden Gates Press 1993, Sun Chalice 2003, Skylight Press 2012.

the odd poisoned spider – all very human overlays of course. I could have got a bit hooked on it at the time and I suspect I may have been warned off by one who knew me better than I knew myself! Who knows?

In a rather "gelical" phrase, "I claim everything for Christ." It is an expression they seem to be able to relate to and it has the advantage of being the plain truth as well. Nice to see the Tarot in its proper place.

The other book that I sent him was *An Introduction to Ritual Magic*, (Thoth Publications, 1997), an attempt on my part to drag this sinister sounding subject out of the dog house and present what it could and should be in terms of a valid and valuable spiritual discipline and way of service.

It was based on a series of articles that Dion Fortune had contributed to the *Inner Light Magazine* over the years and which I had later republished in *New Dimensions*. In this collected edition I added to each of Dion Fortune's articles a chapter of my own to bring things up to date and give practical examples, worked by my group. This included a major one on the Chapels of Remembrance, (an extension of the abbey in *The Abbey Papers*), for the repose of souls disrupted by war – whether victims of conscience; innocent victims; or those utterly smashed physically and mentally by their experience; together with the pacification of flashpoints of human conflict. Much of this had necessitated going to France, visiting war graves and battle fields along the Western Front, particularly the town of Albert, once known as the Lourdes of the North, which had a particularly strong dedication to the Virgin and Child.

My daughter Rebecca played a major role in this, when only a student in my group, who experienced a contact with one of the "three canny lads" (to use Tony Duncan's phrase), who had perished at Ypres in 1916, who went on to inspire a play about himself, *This Wretched Splendour*, which within a few months had had professional and amateur productions in London and Cheltenham, and attracted enthusiastic press reviews.[14]

Tony Duncan's response to *An Introduction to Ritual Magic*, which encapsulated much of this, was equally enthusiastic.

> Many thanks indeed for that magnificent book which I had difficulty in putting down. A most successful "double act" and, as you realized in the

---

14 The script of *This Wretched Splendour* by Rebecca Wilby was published by Skylight Press in 2010.

doing of it, a necessary one which gave the whole thing a completeness and a character which it could not otherwise have had.

It seems to me to represent a fulfilment of White Magic, a discovery of *its right intention* in that what is described is a desire to participate in the Divine Compassion which is what all true Intercession is about. And we proclaim belief in the Communion of Saints – Saints rightly understood in the Pauline sense, not in the Heavenly Athenaeum sense! – so it seems odd to shy away from them as if they are "not quite nice!" I gained a great deal from the book, it is very mind-clearing and also parts of it are very *apropos* in respect of my own current Inner Employments.

It is a thousand pities that so many words are so "loaded" that they can't be used in ordinary conversation any more. (The lovely old English word of my youth – Gay – comes to mind.) The "occult" is getting so open that it really isn't "occult" any more – thank goodness. But the word is unusable in any conversation with "The Reformation" in any of its manifestations; so, alas! is "magic". All is prejudged by the fears of ignorance – compounded with encounters with the badly burned fingers of the dabbler and the nasty psychological wounds of the gross and irresponsible mis-user, both of whom tend to come running to the Vicar for help. One can end up seeing nothing but sickness, therefore everything must be sick – sort of thing! And one knows only too well one's own temptations to misuse!

But no more of these dolours! The thing to do is to get on with the truth and to follow the vocations given as fully and as faithfully as possible. Magic is, I am quite sure, a true vocation for the comparatively few, but – OK – it is a true vocation none the less. Not my own, quite, but I am close enough to have respect and understanding for it and particularly when it finds the kind of fulfilment that your book, and the intention of the Workings manifestly describe. What matters is to get cracking with our Intercession – enter ever more deeply into the Divine Compassion of self-forgetfulness in other words – be it done ritually or in any other way. As they put it in these parts – "Gang on, Hinny!" Time itself may be shorter than we think.

The informant he earlier referred to in connection with waiting twenty years for a work to be published was the Angel in his book *The Sword in the Sun*. This long wait was now miraculously resolved by the intervention of Coleston Brown (also known as Mark Whitehead), who had launched his own publishing imprint, Sun Chalice Books, in California. As well as publishing an important work of his own, *Patterns in Magical Christianity*, and a few titles of mine, he spent the next ten years bringing out a whole series of Tony Duncan's works, beginning with a re-issue of *The Lord of the Dance* and the long delayed angelic conversation *The Sword in the Sun*, moving on to a number of new titles: *The Temple of the Spirit, The Way of Transcendence, A New Heaven and a New Earth, Faversham's Dream* (a novel),[15] *The Forgotten Faith* (an historical account of Celtic saints) and *The Tao of Christ* (the consequence of his studies of Chinese spirituality when a soldier in the Far East).

This consequently led Tony Duncan to write to me that "this retirement thing" was quite hard work, and that he functioned most happily as an itinerant hedge-priest on Sundays, or filling in for local clergy, occasionally touching base back home in Corbridge. The "writing thing" was going apace – he had all manner of irons in fires all over the place and his new computer was kept red hot with it all. He could hardly credit the fact that he had no fewer than seven publishing agreements with Sun Chalice on file.

However, all this did not prevent him from issuing another couple of home produced booklets of poems, *A Bunch of Wild Flowers* and *Some Verses for my Friends*.

---

15 Reissued by Skylight Press, 2011.

One opened with very much the type of poem one would expect from anyone approaching senior citizenship on looking into the shaving mirror each morning, and with which being of much the same age within a few weeks, I could find common ground!

The Man in the Mirror

Who is this fellow thus regarding me?
A man time-scarred in visage, stern of eye.
I know him not; an older man is he.
Myself am young, and ever young am I;
youth's fancies and desires burn in my heart
and in my loins. Such things he cannot know
for they are past for him, he is too old
and set now in his ways, has drawn apart
and has forgotten. Say, it must be so;
I see it in his face, his tale is told!

These four or five years since, that man has gone
who was my mirror-image, so to speak.
And now he has withdrawn from me; gone on
I know not where. And his replacement, bleak
and greying, stands before me now, and shaves,
and brushes somewhat thinner hair than mine.
I go my way and he goes his, to die
perhaps! Yet times I have a glimpse that saves,
that reconciles us even. Strange! No line
is altered, just compassion in his eye.

For I am young, and he is older now
and understands; betrays a gravity
becoming to his years; will not allow,
as unbecoming, my depravity
of mind, the curse of immaturity.
For I am young and kick against the truth
he represents. Yet still we may be one,
for his compassion speaks of a security
transcending time; of an eternal youth
transcending age, and in my youth begun!

But all was not a looking back. And the positive experience with Sun Chalice had given him a new self confidence I think, as regards his writing, and at the turn of the millennium had begun a more ambitious line of publishing himself, with a series of professionally printed and bound little books of his poetry – *Love Germinates* in 2001, *Black Thorn Winter* in 2002, *Of Toads and Men* in 2003, with a fourth planned to complete the series. Apart from specialist small presses poetry is not easily published, let alone sold. And there is indeed an awful lot written of somewhat inferior quality. However, it seemed to me that Tony Duncan's work could not be easily dismissed as the much despised "vanity publishing". For I recall that, back in Parkend, I had introduced him to the established poet and Blake and Yeats scholar Kathleen Raine who was much impressed with his work – "minor, of course," she added, but coming from someone as rigorous as Kathleen Raine that was praise indeed! And speaking for myself I often found his poetry spoke to me more deeply and persuasively than his prose or conversation.

He covered quite a range of course, from deeply mystical work through to light verse that included personal and social comment that was extremely perceptive that could range from the gently ironic to the savage. As for instance in this comment on war.

Victims

Four bright young lads, or was it five,
turned from their target, let all go.
Their five bombs burst; were still alive
but not quite all. Long years ago
the corner shop, hit, tumbled down.
The mains were fractured; those not dead
from bricks and rubble overhead
were slowly gassed or left to drown.

The five lads made it back to base,
I hope, and slept, and phoned their wives.
I cannot know nor judge the case.
How many later lost their lives?
How many, at the last, returned
from long captivity and war
and searched long for a lost front door
to find their wives and children burned?

Or this observation in so-called times of peace.

El Novio de la Muerte

The Bodyguard. Five hundred pounds an hour
and gives the orders. Highly trained to look;
instant reactions, cold; a man of power
and trained to kill; has killed, nor brought to book
(the dead were only Irish); served the Queen
but now discharged. On hire, but at a price,
to rich potential targets who think twice
and seek protection; saved by all he's been.

Defined by death, in every move he makes,
thinks Everyman a killer; this his trade,
his world is psychopathic and it takes
one highly trained as him lest it invade
the diamond-dripping Gulf Princess, or seems,
to portly international business, stark;
to pornographic publishers, too dark!
I'd like his fee! I would not want his dreams.

Or closer to home, the lineaments of a personal tragedy played out behind a façade of social acceptability.

The Two Masks

Chaos and dogs, and laughter too;
dear friends of thirty years and more
we loved so well yet hardly knew
for, when that ever-open door
closed on the fresh air and the sun,
what losing battles then were fought
all out of sight of us, who thought
their dear disfunctionality such fun!

Clouds gathered with the passing years.
No whit less dear, the tensions grew;
past unresolved and present fears.
We laughed and loved and prayed, but knew
that only two could take that strain.
She broke and, of a sudden, died.
He lived in darkness, quite beside
Himself with rage, and died insane.

But he was also capable of a lighter note, albeit with a touch of gentle satire, and close observation of country sports.

THE BOXING DAY MEET

It's Boxing Day. The Hunt will meet.
Groups stand about the market square
with cameras. Some, with placards, there
to protest. In a nearby street
police read papers in their vans,
parked poised and ready, just in case;
all privy to who knows what plans;
prepared to field a second chase.

A girl, clip-clopping on a mare,
wax-jacketed, with merry eyes
and tightly, costly jodhpured thighs,
rides down the hill, the first to bear
the placard-wielders' dumb reproach;
but may not notice, waits for friends.
The Hunt Protesters, in a coach,
likewise awaited at road ends.

So "Peace on Earth" gives place to rage;
two ways of life, opaque to each,
with minds beyond each other's reach.
The "relics of a bygone age"
to be abolished and forbid
in righteousness but, motives blurred,
social resentments hardly hid.
A fox would find the thing absurd.

WILDFOWLING

The hunting instinct: gone completely mad
and socially exalted in good men
and kind; nor murderous, nor cruel, nor bad
but mad to kill, and kill, and kill again!

God's creatures, beautiful, mysterious,
they blow to pieces with a sporting gun;
describe themselves as "Sportsmen!" Serious,
as if each slaughter were a battle won.

Some, sated, and with passing years mature,
turn Naturalist and love what they have slain.
Write books, take up photography, endure
long hours in hides. The rest: they kill again.

Now done my sermon! 'Tis the preacher's lot
to eat with relish what these "Sportsmen" shot!

But I found an intriguing feature of his work to cover memories of childhood and early adolescence. This first one also making an important psychological point about the function of the imagination and intuition that tends to be abandoned in adult life.

NURSERY WISDOM

An only child, a lonely child,
I lived within a boundless mind.
The adult world surrounding, smiled,
but few there were of my own kind.
I found that life projected brings
full flock of friends, all of them fond
for, given life, they will respond
with love for love, these nursery things.

Now I am old I see it clear.
Imagination, unrestrained,
respects realities and feels no fear,
is happy to leave unexplained
that sense of "something in the air":
accepts, relates with utmost ease
to what the intuition sees:
the *Presence* of a teddy-bear.

And the increasing sense of iron bars about the schoolboy soul:

THE LONER

Time was when I escaped from school
as from a dungeon's iron bars
and let imagination rule
and ran amok among the stars.
I'd re-create the universe
and live in my ecstatic mind
'til snared again, back to the grind;
imagination quelled – or worse.

My inner worlds would open wide
and, flying free as any bird
from worlds within to world outside,
adult's constraints would seem absurd;
imagination was the norm.
The adult world would then intrude;
I'd stand accused of being rude!
Then school – and learning to conform.

The attempts in adolescence to become a man:

THE SHOT

One time, in time long past, I'd look and lust
down the long barrel of a sporting gun
and prove my early manhood with a single shot;
bow to applause without, within. No more.
I worship now in wonderment, my distance keep.
My quarry has defeated me, settled the score.

Now of that grace and gentleness I seek the trust,
bewildered now by beauty, a new life begun.
The past is gathered, nor rejected nor forgot,
but true to Nature whose own Truth is found in Grace.
So is the mystery in me; desire most deep
to look into my quarry's eyes, meet face to face.

And to come to terms with being a man:

MEN

Male company I love, but not a crowd
self-consciously male-bonding, or a pack
unconsciously conforming, brash and loud,
colliding into bars the pints to stack.
Nor in myself do I discern a lack
demanding brotherhood and rites arcane
to plug the gaps within, or guard my back
from stabbing, or discreet advantage gain.
The men whom I admire are, in the main,
grown up from boys not best beloved by schools,
but loners were and are, and different; sane
yet mad enough to disregard the rules;
grown up to manhood – then grown on again;
forever boys, and child-like. These are *men!*

And then, beyond all, the call of his mystical vocation.

The One Essential Me

A myriad stars am I; a universe.
The galaxies of endless inner space –
until such time as they shall then disperse –
my mystery expressing, held in place.
Within the Mind, created mind am I
and live its Life and of its thoughts partaking;
a microcosm underneath the sky,
deep-mired in mud, my universe creating.

Within the endless Void, non-void am I,
who am brim-full of voidness, so to find
my purpose, so to live and so to die;
expression of the Character of Mind.
So shall emerge one essential "Me"
when, thus expressed, I love itself shall be.

Memories

An angel, so the legend goes, wipes clean
omniscience from out the human mind
as it descends to be conceived and born on Earth.
Omniscience to ignorance! A strife to learn
to know, to understand, and in the end to love,
identified with Wisdom and with Earth; both one
within the ape-and-angel unity. God's plan
for harvesting, fulfilling, through the mind of Man.

Some angels wink, not over-keen
to reach into the corners or to look to find
remaining traces. So are brought to birth
lives lost in longing, hearts that yearn
for once-known, half-remembered things above,
beyond, other and real. The Quest begun,
consumes and drives, demands them 'till they die
and see, and Live! And such a one am I.

The last time I heard from Tony Duncan was on an up-beat note on 10th December 2002:

> Two great truths have manifested this year. The first is that the older one gets the quicker the time passes. The second is that, being retired, there is no possibility of ever finding time to go to work! Nevertheless I seem to keep my hand in, looking after priestless parishes during interregna (and then slightly resenting the arrival of the new incumbent!) and, as always, scribbling.
>
> The family are in good order, thank God and we have had a lively year. Helga's little fashion business is a real blessing and on all kinds of levels. Our circle of friends and acquaintances is perpetually expanding, she is very fulfilled, doing something she is exceedingly good at, the Bank Manager is mollified, we can afford holidays and a few extras – and I get to flirt with a lot of pretty women! Long may it last.

Tony proudly presenting his raised bed wall with built-in coffee-tables, Corbridge, April 2003.

But alas it did not last. A few months later, shortly before his 73rd birthday he died suddenly at home, on 8th May 2003. His heart just stopped beating. He had lived to the full to the last minute, said Helga, and died clutching a handkerchief. A wonderful death for him but a tremendous shock for those left behind.

It seems appropriate to end this account of his life with the poem of his with which we began.

ME

Myself (of which I make so great
a fuss) is a mere, brittle spike
of consciousness on the circumference of being;
a tiny terminal of an unplumbed depth.

Before I flew, a midnight lark
into the lamplit song, I was a potency;
a tiny "not yet" waiting for the act,
the pre-set accident of chain-reacting love.

And now I stand and bristle to my fall,
a tensioner of seen and the unseen,
forging new links to the inherent chain,

waking new eyes to glory in diminishment,
as my sand runs in the antipodean glass
and soars into the starlit depths.

His sand may have run in the antipodean glass, but his soul surely soars into the starlit depths.

9

OF TOADS AND MEN

H<small>IS FRIENDS</small>, relations and parishioners past and present contributed to a memorial window for him in St Helen's church at Whitley Mill. It seems to me that a window was a fitting image for one who was a window into and out of the world in more ways than one. For me though, the title of his last little booklet of poems, and the poem within it, sums up the essence of the humanity of the man. One who had "an understanding dignified and rare."

A Ballad of Toads and Men

As I stepped out along the rough sea wall
which bounds the Wash, where once the tide had flowed
in Norman times to Snettisham, to fall
in winter floods across the coastal road,
and crunched the shingle underfoot, and strode,
lungs salt and spiced up sharp with good sea air,
released from duties and without a care,
I spied – stopped suddenly and stooped – a Toad!

An urgent hop and flop, a leap and fall,
a *pranayama* in reptilian mode,
a "lotus posture", prone, as if to crawl.
A countenance upon which was bestowed
a meditative cast as if it "knowed,"
but knew not quite what I was doing there;
regarded my approach as hardly fair
and far removed from its own Highway Code.

Of Toads and Men

I stopped to pass the time of day and all
was well between us and, discreet, I showed
my interest in photography withal
to take his likeness; and the sporting Toad,
six inches from my lens, breathed hard, swallowed,
and fixed the shutter with a beady stare
and bade the thing come nearer if it dare!
And held his ground 'till all my gear was stowed.

We parted friends, and he to his abode
and I to mine departed. Both had there
arrived, as Toad to Man and Man to Toad,
at understanding, dignified and rare.

The memorial window at Whitley Mill

As to our friendship and our work together, it seemed, like the pillars of the temple of wisdom, to make some kind of gateway, to generate some kind of dynamic, from which we both emerged changed, and in different ways enriched.

One of his poems may have been written with this relationship in mind. Mind you, it may well have been written to some entirely different person. It is a late poem and I never had a chance to ask him. But it fits quite well.

My own perceived background when we first met being part of a Neoplatonic cosmos of far flung spirits – his own an equally cosmic but more personal and Christological view. Thus the contrast between Christ and Qabalah, which in the end, rightly viewed, with the mind in the heart, might well be regarded as mirror images, one of the other. Any apparent distortion being the result of our own defective sight.

To a Soul-Friend

I know, yet know not who you are,
or who you have been, who you yet may be.
As if from one long-distant star
we're come, are met on Earth, to be
that which we represent eternally.

We live our given earthly lives
in Love, yet not in love to possess
as, husbands, lovers or as wives,
yet distant, do not love the less,
abiding in a mutual tenderness.

For old we are and practised long;
are both embarked on one eternal Quest,
each here to make the other strong
until each enter into rest,
thence to abide, each in the other blest.

Yet, lest we take each other's part
in each as of some great significance,
'tis but the workings of the Heart
and Mind of Christ; not our own chance
but one small measure of the One Great Dance.

Index of Poems

Absurdity, An	125
Aches and Pains	32
Aerodrome, The	118
Aldershot	152
All Things Converge	194
A Moment Later and I Might Have Seen Them…	18
Anniversary, The	185
Ascension Day in the Garden	162
At Dead of Night	122
Atholl Brigade at Culloden	111
A.U. XI, The	196
Auntie	153
Auschwitz and Dresden	139
Balaam's Dog	55
Ballad of Toads and Men, A	214
Becoming	195
Blackthorn Winter	148
Bonny Lass, The	76
Boxing Day Meet, The	207
Brush, The	15
Castle of the Heart, The	189
Celebrant, The	158
Celebration of Cats Eternal, A	120
Charmed Ring, The	46
Chichester: the Theological College	146
Child of Earth, The	191
Child of Heaven, The	192
Cold, Wet April, A	160
Conspiracy	77
Contemplation	33
Crying for the Moon	154
Curse, The	48
Day Room, The	176
Dear Aquinas SV	164
Development	152
Devil Water, The	145
Dog	96
Elizabeth	177
Elmbury Abbey	9

Index of Poems

E.T. 1st XI, The	197
E.T. 2nd XI, The	198
Eternity	74
Exorcism, An	45
Faerie	147
Fierce Prayers	59
Finding and Losing	190
Forty Years On	165
Friendship of Faerie	66
Gardener, The	147
Ghosts	16
Girl at the Check-Out, The	170
Glimpse of Reality, A	123
Gnostic, The	40
Grove, The	94
Growing Pains	106
Healer, The	177
Healer and Patient	100
He Came, as he Said…	70
Helvelyn	134
Highnam	58
High Places	161
Holy Matrimony	172
Hospital Chaplain, The	175
How Many Heavens?	195
Husband's View of a Pedestrian Precinct, A	173
I Am	21
I Cried Aloud	69
I Know a Man…	41
Image of God, The	131
Indigo Unheralded	27
Industrial Archaeology	27
In Seremban	151
Joy in Heaven	45
Kabbalah	38
Lakeland Fells, The	108
Life	150
Linhope Spout	161
Little Church and Churchyard at Rudford, The	72
Llanfihangel	29
Logres	128
Loner, The	209
Love Germinates	146
Love Lies Bleeding	170

Lover Within, The	130
Love's Journeyings	193
Love, Youth and Age	168
Lüneburger Heide, Die	150
Magic	12
Man in the Mirror, The	204
Mass Priest, The	102
May Hill	25
Me	213
Meaning	42
Meditation Group, The	55
Melissa	169
Memories	211
Men	210
Miah	167
Monastery, The	132
Monks of Tewkesbury	22
Month of March, The	159
My Lover Called Me from the Bed of Dawn	20
My Native Land	112
My Neighbour	131
Mystic Mystified, The	104
Nancy's Helen	167
Nirvana Point	35
Novio de la Muerte, El	206
Nursery Wisdom	208
Oakenhill Wood	74
Observations of a Gentleman Friend	174
Ode for St. Augustine's Day	163
"Of the Earth, Earthy"	130
Old Orchard, The	30
Old Workings	26
One Essential Me, The	211
On the Press of Irrelevance	104
Over the Hill	17
Paps of Jura, The	108
Parish Priest Retired, The	179
Path-Working	38
Peace	177
Poor Moses	20
Portrait of a Predecessor	187
Priest, The	106
Priesthood of Man, The	135
Priest in Retrospect, The	102

Index of Poems

Prophet, The	178
Prophet in Frustration, The	103
Prophet's Reward, A	125
Prospect of a Garden Party	180
Rectory, The	186
Red Bricks in the Grey of Dawn	75
Root and Rock	109
St John's Church, Acklington	115
St John's Church Newcastle upon Tyne	85
Seeker, The	40
Shot, The	210
Sick Communion	19
Silence in Heaven	107
Sister	133
Spanish Girls	171
Sphere of Silence, The	188
Spinal Ward, The	176
Spiritual Warfare	105
Squire's Pew	84
Three Towns	95
Ticket Hop	119
To an Urgently Aspiring Mystic	39
To a Soul-Friend	216
To the Guardian Angel	122
To the Mother of God	133
Transfiguration	165
Travelling Light	174
Two Dimensions	39
Two Masks, The	206
Understanding	41
Upon May Hill	24
Victims	205
Visitation, A	121
Warkworth Hermitage	114
Waves and Vibrations	92
West End	94
West of the Severn	23
Whitley Vicarage	144
Wildfowling	208
Wild Goose Flighted, The	179
Witchcraft	69
Yellow Socks	16